# G-Man For All Seasons

## Seasons

### HBCU 3 Sports Superstar

### Touchdowns, Dunks and Jumps

## Andrew "Poncho" Glover

**\*SWAC and HBCU Historic Achievement**
**\*Conquering the NFL**

Published By: Books For Athletes
www.BooksForAthletes.com

# Table of Contents

# Introduction

S ports and I developed a love-love relationship early on. Like romantic love, we entered into an unspoken agreement, and were whisked away into the land of oblivion hoping we would never come out. We put forth our best version of ourselves to maintain that invigorating feeling love produces. I was entirely overtaken by a feeling that is indescribable. At the age of 11, I did not have the language to express what I was feeling, but all I knew was I did not want this feeling to end. While living on Green Acres the pages to our love story started to be written. I can still feel that sinking feeling in my tiny chest and the joy that percolated down my spine when I saw it. It was like admiring a beautiful woman, painting, car, or flower for the first time and being overtaken by its beauty. Basketball, football, track, baseball, or any sport for that matter, I was head over hills. That day I took love by the hand and let it lead me to a lifetime of happiness, sadness, compromise, triumphs, disappointments, wins and ascension. Some life moments are etched in our minds forever, and the beginning of this love story is one of them for me.

Moving at least seven times during my childhood was a traumatic experience. I could not truly call a place home until we moved to Green Acres. It was named Green Acres because all the homes on the block were painted green. A community man built homes and rented them to families in the area. He also employed many people in the neighborhood to help with the maintenance of the community. My mom rented one of the green homes. It was a three-bedroom, one bathroom home, on a dead end street, in a small town named Geismar. This was my most memorable childhood home. This is when my life began. This is when I knew what it felt like to love. Please do not misunderstand me, I knew what love was. My mom showed us love unconditionally in how she raised me and my siblings. Our mom was a proud woman and raised us to be respectful, disciplined and hardworking individuals. She poured all her strength, sacrifices, hard work, and know-how into loving us.

While living on Green Acres, we would all commune in the kitchen, the heart of the home or on the front porch overlooking the dead end street. If you looked up and down the street, you would be sure to spot plenty of kids who wanted to play and had the same interests as I did. Guaranteed you could always find someone to play with outside. Geismar was filled with children who had lots of dreams, just like me. My family loved sports. I mean *really* loved sports, to the point where they knew names, stats, salaries, colleges they attended, plays from previous games, and all of the behind the scenes drama. The conversation even shifted to the coaching style and decisions of the coaches. We were locked in. We then found ourselves imagining what we would do with all the money, fame, power and influence the players had. Boy did our imaginations run wild and far from the tiny community of Green Acres, far, far away from Ascension

Parish. Those conversations were tantalizing. New Orleans, "The Who Dat Nation" and the Dallas Cowboys were the teams that we talked about mostly. It was because they were close to us geographically. You always root for the home team, everyone knew that. That is the golden rule.

One day, out of nowhere, it seemed like my love heightened for sports. gathering around and talking about sports was a common occurrence for my family. I reckon like in romantic relationships, one day you're living your life and the next minute you're hopelessly in love. As I look back at the time on Green Acres, I can attest to it feeling safe. Feeling safe as a child is necessary for proper development. When you feel safe you can love and let your guards down. This is what happened to me on Green Acres, in that small, green house, on that dead end block in Geismar, Louisiana. I was finally home.

The love-struck young Poncho dove deep, headfirst into this relationship. All sorts of sports and athletes were now my focus. It was like I became hyper focused on sports quickly. I'd nestle in front of the tiny 24 inch black and white television with an old wire hanger for the antenna and just watch athletes. They mesmerized me with their physical abilities. Not to mention all of the fanfare. Thousands of people cheering and standing up while they played their best game was exhilarating to watch. I'd imagine it was even more liberating to experience. With only one TV in the house, there was never really any debate on what we were watching because the family always wanted to watch a game, or something sports related. It was a win-win situation for me.

The sports documentaries were my favorite. It was getting to know the athletes outside of their comfort zone that intrigued me the most. The players' work ethics, childhood experiences, families and achievements on and off the field or court was what kept me sitting in front of that black and white TV for hours upon hours.

Jesse Owens, an African American track and field star was one of my heroes. I watched a documentary about him and was amazed by his story. I learned that he grew up in Alabama. where his family were sharecroppers. He and his 9 siblings had to help their family pick cotton. He was two generations away from slavery, his grandparents were slaves. It was astonishing to learn that the same hands that picked cotton in the field, under the blazing sun, would later ignite the Olympic eternal flame, winning 4 gold medals and changing history in 1936. Then I saw a documentary on Jim Thorpe, another magnificent athlete. Thorpe, an American Indian, born a twin, was raised on a farm. It was documented that he was not tall or big in stature but worked extremely hard and excelled in multiple sports. Thorpe was a superstar athlete in every sense of the word. He was also an Olympic champion, played professional football, baseball and basketball and was considered one of the most versatile athletes in modern day sports. Learning about these two impressive men motivated me to watch various sports. The competitiveness displayed by these men allowed them to perform at high levels and be great. As a kid, I was entranced by all of the adulation that fans were giving these players. Love was preparing me to eventually be married to the game. For me sports was becoming my true love.

Watching Dr. J and Wilt Chamberlain in their prime was unmatched. These guys single-handedly made basketball one of my favorites to watch. Dr. J revolutionized the slam dunk. This man had moves no one had seen before. Then I learned that Dr. J was raised by a single mom. This fact woke up something in me. Observing these modern day heroes and realizing their stories mirrored my life in more ways than one. This made me believe I could one day achieve the same dreams.

Wilt Chamberlain appeared larger than life on our small bubble screen TV, standing at 7'1. I was a fan as I watched him break every record imaginable. Pure love had officially engulfed me. How can a kid watch all of this greatness and not work on his own game? Work on my game is exactly what I did. Practicing in our front yard with my brothers and other neighborhood kids was when a great athlete began to form, not only on the courts but in my heart. It was fulfilling but only for the moment, I wanted to be part of a team. When you love something, you want to share that love and show it off to everyone. I wanted to show off my skill and dedication and love to the world. I wanted to express my love at a high level. I needed to join a team with people that felt the same way I did

# Dedication

I have been blessed beyond anything I could have ever imagined. I could not have accomplished any of my goals and aspirations without the guidance of my Lord and Savior, Jesus Christ. I dedicate my life and this book to my wife, Mary, and my children, PJ, Christon, and Alex; they have served as inspiration for me to achieve more than I thought I was capable of. They provide the fire that burns in me to be better today than I was yesterday. Lastly, I want to dedicate this book to the student athletes that look like me, come from where I came from, and have been told that they will not succeed. Don't allow anyone to define who you aspire to be as a student athlete.

# Acknowledgments

I would like to thank God for entrusting me with the gifts and talents he has blessed me with. My greatest joy as an athlete has been winning three championships while representing the greatest HBCU in the nation, THE Grambling State University.

I would like to thank my mother, the late Mary Ann Glover Coco, for bringing me into this world, loving me, and praying over me. She is responsible for me being the man that God intended for me to be.

I would like to thank my mother-in-law, the late Barbara J. Harris, for teaching me about giving and philanthropy. She lived her life by giving to others and expecting nothing in return. Because of her vision, we partnered together to start our nonprofit, Glover House.

My wife, Mary: You are the inspiration that has elevated me to places I have only dreamed about. Your love and support have empowered this journey for 35 years and beyond. I am forever thankful and grateful to share my life with you.

To my children, PJ, Christon, and Alex: I am so proud of the young adults you have become. Keep living, loving, and being happy. Y'all make me feel like the luckiest father in the world.

To my brothers and sisters: thank you for the prayers and good gestures along the way. God has truly been faithful to our family.

To the Sharper Family: thank you for your selfless act of welcoming me into your household and treating me like family. You help steer my path, teaching me discipline and hard work. Georgia Mae Sharper's love and spirit will continue to watch over us every day. I know we are making her proud.

To the Geismar family: I thank you for sharing Mr. Bubber and Ms. Mickey with a young boy that needed guidance and unconditional love. Mr. Bubber was an instrumental part of my development as a man. He was a true visionary who believed in me and my abilities to become a great student athlete. He helped nurture my talents from adolescence to the NFL and beyond.

Thank you to my coaches, friends, family, and teammates. I am extremely grateful for the motivation, support, and time spent competing and building lifelong relationships on my journey.

I would like to send out a special shout out to my G Men Nation brothers; you are a family that I did not know I needed until I stepped foot on Grambling State University's Campus. You held me accountable then, and you continued to raise the bar and make all impossible dreams seem possible.

# CHAPTER 1

# The Confirmation Letter

In January 1999, after a great practice preparing for our NFC championship game, I entered the locker room as a Minnesota Viking. This was the game that would determine if we were going to the Super Bowl, so the energy in the locker room was high. Each time I entered the locker room, I thanked God for another day in paradise. I was amazed at what God had allowed. The man I had become was a testament to all the work I had done internally. I chatted with a few of my teammates and went to my locker as usual. I'm tired, sweaty, and excited about my place in life, and all I wanted was a shower, food, rest, and to see my family. To my surprise, there was a FedEx envelope at my locker. After carefully observing all the players talking and laughing, no one noticed I had received an envelope. I then noticed no one else had received a letter either. I'm apprehensive to open it, especially seeing who it was from, but it was addressed to me as Andrew "PONCHO" Glover. As I tore open the envelope, I saw the name Al Davis. The letter was from the then-Oakland

Raiders owner and Godfather of the NFL, the highly esteemed Al Davis. Al Davis was a mover and shaker in the NFL and was revered by many. I was perplexed as to why he would be sending *me* a letter, as we did not end my six-year Raiders career on the best note in 1996. All I kept wondering was what he could have wanted. His vision for me did not align with what I desired, and I was released from the Oakland Raiders, the Silver and Black. In hindsight, I'm proud that I stood my ground and refused to accept what was being offered contractually. My values would not allow me to concede and just roll with the punches. The situation was sticky. My agent could not get me secured with another team; no one was biting. We fished fervently for quite some time before signing back with the team. The original offer of $600,000 was now $400,000. That was a tough space to be in, but I persevered. I knew my time as a Raider was coming to an end. The team locker room I'm currently sitting in, reading this handwritten note, from one of the most powerful men in the NFL. Al Davis is someone a NFL player wanted on their side. Life has an elusive way of bringing things back full circle. The note read:

*Dear Andrew:*

*While "The Dream" never became a reality with the "The Silver & Black," you are on the threshold of an unbelievable experience. It has been a long journey since 1991, when the skinny wide receiver (TE) was drafted out of Grambling, and you deserve congratulations for your fortitude, towering courage, and commitment. Our paths will cross sometime in the future. I admire your loyalty.*

*Most Sincerely, and Regards to Your Family*
*Al Davis*

I re-read the note several times and never spoke a word to any of the other players in that locker room. This was a sacred moment for me. Flashbacks of Al and my last conversation started replaying in my head. Initially, I was surprised and shocked. This note was going to take some processing on my part. The small note validated so many of my feelings of inadequacy that I had endured as a Raider. This note started to soften my heart as he opened up about his thoughts about me. Al Davis was watching me well after I had left his organization, unbeknownst to me. He was looking at me from afar. He was acknowledging the places I had ascended after being dismissed by his organization. This small piece of Oakland Raider embroidery paper was more valuable than the $90,000 contract Al Davis gave me when I was drafted in 1991. As a matter of fact, it was invaluable. This is how precious this note was to me. The key points that were mentioned in that note hit home for me. He mentioned my being loyal. Davis was referring to the fact that I was loyal to the Raiders despite having had opportunities to play professional basketball as well. My skill sets were impeccable in both sports, as I played both sports in High School and at the collegiate level. However, I felt like I needed to put all my effort into one sport. There were no advisors around me saying I could be a dual-professional sports player. The buzz about how well a basketball player I was surfaced in newspaper articles, well after a year of being a Raider. The right influence can change the trajectory of one's life. The absence of the right influence can change the trajectory of one's life, as well. This was my opportunity to do something monumental in the history of sports, but I settled for being a football player. Wrestling with my own insecurities caused me to choose the NFL. Had I done both sports, it would have more than likely taken away from my football skills, but that remains to be seen. I can speculate all day, but I will never know that aspect of my basketball talent.

I became a starter after 3 years with the team. Even with all the new players that were brought in to play my position, I fought to keep my position and never even peered on the other side of the fence to entertain a basketball opportunity. Davis may have already had a preconceived notion that I was going to try and do both sports. Bo Jackson, the only professional US player in history to be named an All-Star in the NFL and MLB, was allowed to do it, but I got in my own way. Bo Jackson ended up having an injury that ended his career. When he speaks about loyalty, he's speaking of my loyalty to football at my own personal expense.

Davis recognized the dedication I put in to become a better football player. What I accomplished statistically in six years with his organization only took me three years to accomplish with the Vikings. I eclipsed all that hard work in LA and was able to accomplish more while in Minnesota. I was the third-leading receiver on the highest-scoring offense in the history of the NFL. During this time, we were in our playoff season. Coming in not knowing any of the guys and gelling with the team, starting at the back of the line and working my way up to the front, was unheard of. Hard work, effort, grit, and tenacity had only taken me so far in LA. I did everything that was asked and more than was required of me as a Raider. In return, my desires were not met.

Nonetheless, I worked hard, and all my hard work was not in vain in LA because I came to Minnesota and was rewarded with a contract I was proud of.

I'm eternally grateful for the LA Raiders opportunity in 1991. I can appreciate the investment in me to develop me, but the payoff was not intended for LA; it was intended for Minnesota. I truly believe Al Davis sensed he fumbled a great player prematurely, and the letter was a cryptic reflection of that.

This line from the letter: *While "The Dream" never became a reality with "The Silver & Black," you are on the threshold of an unbelievable experience.* Showed me that he had been watching from afar.

Unlike now, in 2023, NFL contracts worked differently from when I was drafted in 1991, over 30 years ago. Contracts are now guaranteed; that was not an option during my time. After being drafted, you still must go and compete for a spot on the 47-man roster. Sitting here in this locker room amongst all these phenomenal players allowed me to reflect on how I landed here, after now being in the NFL for eight years, reading this letter, wearing this uniform, and living this extremely blessed life that has afforded me the opportunity to help many people.

This journey we're about to embark on is sincerely about a man with a fervent love for sports, especially football. A man who worked tirelessly, a dreamer who was unwavering in his desire to see it manifest despite all the obstacles before him.

In football, we yell "HIKE" to alert the team that the ball is being snapped. I'm yelling *hike*, so you can get ready for this story. The question remains: what are you going to do with the information? How will you apply it to your life to learn, lead, and live in a way that is exemplary for others so that they score? You're on offense.

### *HIKE!*

# CHAPTER 2

# Humble Beginnings

## *G Man for Life!*

Because when you love something, like I loved sports, you put forth your best effort; mediocrity is not in your vocabulary. Especially growing up with the kind of mother I had. My mother was a no-nonsense woman who believed that hard work was the only way to be successful. Although my mother was a single parent raising six children on her own, she always tried to put us in the best positions to achieve.

She desired a better life for us than she was afforded as a child growing up in rural Louisiana. She wanted us to experience and have more than she had growing up. My mother realized early in my childhood that growing up in a community that was close to family was not always a positive atmosphere. She wanted more for us. She wanted to take my siblings and me from an environment where she did not feel we were being nurtured.

She knew we needed to see more than what we had been exposed to, so we moved often. We finally landed in a small town named Gonzales, located in Ascension Parish. This community was located between Baton Rouge and New Orleans, Louisiana. We were across town from most of my family. Ascension Parish was a thriving community with lots of families and burgeoning businesses. We were a tight-knit community where everyone knew everyone. Gonzales was growing at a slow and steady pace. This little slice of hidden heaven was the perfect place to raise a family. We did not have significant race-related issues, but we did have areas that blacks knew to stay clear of. Furthermore, blacks and whites worked together, kids played sports together, and we helped each other as we progressed. The school systems were top-tier, with great leaders, teachers, and coaches who genuinely cared about the town and the children and families in it. All the adults watched out for the kids and corrected or congratulated them according to their behavior. Our town was impactful and made a mark on everyone who was blessed to be a part of it. We were known as the "Jambalaya Capital of the World". There was a Jambalaya festival held every year during Memorial Day weekend. This was a time when all the communities, black and white, would come together to showcase to the nation our love for food and family. The Jambalaya festivals we had in the community were the best. You could smell the spices, seafood, and love put into these dishes from great distances. This was truly a family atmosphere. My mother could not have found a better place for us to live. This town was essential to the man that I would later become.

Mothers are strong. Stronger than they want to be,and as strong as they need to be. Hard work and dedication were taught to me by my mother. She was one of the strongest women I knew. She single-handedly raised six children while providing all of our necessities. She taught my siblings and me that if we wanted to be successful, we would have to work hard. She worked tirelessly to provide for the six of us by taking jobs that most people might think are minuscule, such as restaurants and cleaning hotel rooms. My mom would often work several jobs to make ends meet.

The pay checks were not nearly enough to provide us with any extras. With six hungry bellies to feed and growing kids, she would have to sometimes apply for welfare to fill in the gaps. One thing about my mother is that she did not like to take handouts, so asking for help was difficult for her. She was a proud woman and did what she had to do to provide for us. Mom was very loving, and she was a strict disciplinarian. She had high expectations, holding us accountable for our mistakes while making sure we were on our best behavior in school and out in the community. She provided what she could. We often had to wear hand-me-downs or get clothing from the second-hand store. I grew very fast, so my hand-me-downs to my siblings were still useful. Nothing was wasted.

My biological father was incarcerated when I was young, and because of this, we were not able to develop a proper father-son relationship.

Although my biological father was not in the home, my mother later married, and my stepfather was an integral part of my childhood. It was nice to have a male figure in the home. My stepfather would take me fishing, and we would do things that other fathers and sons would do. Different men in the community would provide me with guidance and mentorship. They would also reprimand me when I needed it. There was so much that my "village of men" taught me. When I was about 11 or 12, I would do odd jobs for money to help my family. I would always do these chores with pride and integrity, always returning on time and always bringing back the correct change. Integrity, I would learn as I matured, was a characteristic trait that would serve me well as an accomplished athlete. News began to spread about young Poncho and his errand-running. I began to get asked to run errands for a man I would later call my Godfather. He would mentor me along with my "village of men". Later, I was invited to his home to live with him and his family, while I attended high school.

## *"Do It, Do It Poncho, Do It"*

In 7th grade, I wanted to play sports, but mom did not have a vehicle to get me to practice, plus she could not afford the registration. Basketball at school was free to all who wanted to participate, but it required basketball shoes, physicals, and transportation to practice. I did not make the basketball team at school. To anyone else, this may have been a huge hurdle, but when there's a will, there is a way. I would not allow my love of sports to be stunted because of my socioeconomic status. Nothing could stop me, and more than anything, it made me work harder. The athletes that made the team had more of a foundation in the game because they participated in little league. They had a huge advantage, but that did not matter to me. My ingenuity kicked in, and I crafted a basketball rim of my own. I found an old bicycle wheel, beat the spokes out of it with a blunt object, perhaps a rock, and then nailed it to the tree in front of my house with two rusted nails. The last obstacle was finding a round object to throw into the makeshift hoop. No backboard, no net, no ball—just a rim and love for the game. In my mind, I was trying to emulate what I had been witnessing on TV from these great players in the NBA. Here I was, the poor kid, practicing my game on a bike rim with anything round that I could find to make shots. I was going to practice to make sure I made that team in the 8th grade. By any means necessary. I practiced every day in the yard before and after school. I was obsessed with being great. The adage "everything you need is already in your hands" was true for me. Grit, willpower, creativity, persistence, and love for the game were all I had; everything else I needed; God would provide along the way.

All the kids at Green Acres began to recognize me. I was always on the playground, I would use what I learned from the older guys to beat the kids my age. On the way to school I'd sit in the front seat of the bus to ensure I got off first so I could get to the sandlot. I was impatient yet full of energy. I would run, trying to be first in line to get to the playground. It never mattered to me that the bus had to pick up other kids in the neighborhood; I wanted to play. My anxiety grew with each kid the bus driver had to stop for. I would grab the seat in front of me or punch it in my desperate anticipation. My buddy nicknamed me "Spaghetti Man" because I was so scrawny with not much to hold me down. Much like the character Scarecrow from The Wizard of Oz. But one thing was certain: after all the practicing, my game was evolving.

Before the bus driver swung the door open, I would jump off the top step so that I could be the first player on the field. Teams were being picked, usually by the kid playing the quarterback position. In hindsight, we were extremely organized for children. We knew which players should play each position, and there was never any resistance from the other kids. We all agreed and played the positions based on ability. My position was wide receiver. It was imperative that I secure a spot on the winning team because my objective was to be the hero each day. I had to get in and make a superhuman play, hoping that it would be the play that won the game. Catching that soft nerf football was just like watching the pro players on our small 24-inch black and white television. As I would catch the ball, in my head I heard the commentator, Howard Cosell, saying, "He's at the 20, the 30, the 40, the 50, the 40, the 30, the 20, the 10, TOUCHDOWN!" But this time it was me catching the pig skin on the turf. The multicolored ball spiraling in the air was beautiful to watch. When thrown correctly, the ball would be easy to snatch out of the air.

As a 12-year-old boy, this was invigorating. For a moment, I knew what those professional players felt like. I wanted to be a part of a team, and I knew that I would one day have that opportunity if I kept working hard.

In the 8th grade, I finally made the basketball team. This was my first year of organized sports. Boy, was I ecstatic and proud! Shooting around with my makeshift basketball rim finally paid off. Young Poncho was right where he belonged, but I had little to no playing experience. My skill set was underdeveloped. The coaches worked with me, and I listened to what was asked of me so that I could get better. Had I focused on what I did not have as opposed to what I did have, I would not have been able to be happy for my teammates when we won. Suiting up to sit on the bench was enough for me. I was extremely grateful for the opportunity, and I was not going to mess it up. This was the first time that I felt accepted, and I loved that feeling. I was finally part of a team. The way I cheered for my teammates during a game, you would have thought I was playing. I had the mentality, "If one of us wins, we all win." After the games, I would dance to entertain my teammates and the fans that attended the games. I was just being silly, and my teammates would gather around me and chant, "Do it, do it, Poncho, do it". Those were the best of times. After the games, they would look for me to do the dance so they could chant. Every time I got the opportunity, I did the dance. It was exhilarating for me. I wanted to do whatever I could to be a part of this team. What I know now is that dancing and entertaining my teammates was the beginning of my growing into an unselfish teammate. This would be one of the characteristics that would help me make my dreams come true. I was part of a team, and I loved it.

*"Do it, do it, Poncho, do it!*

# CHAPTER 3

# **Greatness in Progress**

Lessons learned as a young man about loving a thing to my detriment put things into perspective for me. Initially, it was not made clear until it was almost too late. Being a high school student and 3 sport athlete, came with its own pressures. I can't say that all the attention to my hard work was not addictive. Unfortunately, a touch of arrogance was born out of that. I took up basketball, football, and track and field in high school, and I excelled in all three. I knew that I wanted to create a path for young Poncho that would set me apart. With great talent comes great responsibility. The responsibility part sometimes fell on deaf ears. My focus was athletics.

I loved sports but neglected my academic responsibilities. Loving a thing too much can cause damage when we do not continue to take care of the things that matter in school.

Balance was not a skill I had mastered. It was either all sports or nothing for me. Academics, who needed that—well, apparently me—my negligence in my studies almost cost me my scholarship to Grambling State University.

During high school, I lived with my Godfather and his family. He only had daughters, and my mother thought it would be a great idea for me to learn from him. As a construction worker, farmer, and family man, he had high expectations of me and taught me the value of hard work. He instilled hard work, discipline, patience, and persistence. Being a student of his allowed me to learn all of these trades. One Friday, I stayed out all night after football and planned to sleep in on Saturday to recover from a long night of teenage shenanigans. My Godfather had different plans. He came into my room and ordered me out of bed and to the vegetable fields before sunrise to work. My Friday night lights and games were not important if I could not maintain what I had to do at home. I had to be able to do both to be successful. "*If you hang out with the owls, you got to be able to get up with the chickens,*" is what he would say. This is a theme that I would fumble several times before I finally understood it at Grambling.

My high school career was slowly coming to an end, and my grades were subpar. My grades took a drastic plummet because of my lack of discipline, patience, hard work, and persistence. Had I put in half the effort in academia as I did in sports, I would have thrived. In hindsight, I can now admit that a touch of arrogance had me thinking I was untouchable.

If I was a great athlete, the grade did not matter. Athletics over academics was what I thought. My thought process was completely off. The varsity football coach came to me with a box of letters from colleges all over the country, but since my grades were so poor, it was almost impossible for me to try and catch up with the little time I had left. Embarrassed at what I had done to myself, I worked as hard as I could. Those lessons from my Godfather now make sense. Time was running out. I buckled down to try and turn around my grades as best as possible. However, too much effort was applied too late. With that, I concluded my senior year of high school with barely a 2.3 GPA and a 14 on the ACT exam. Quite naturally, schools were not beating down my door with offers, despite all the major accomplishments I had made in three sports. With those poor grades, there was nothing the schools were excited about putting their hands on. I had not satisfied the minimum requirements to be eligible for my first year of college, let alone play a sport.

However, I was able to pull it off because of great relationships. Great relationships make the difference between night and day. As a high school student, I had built another thriving and beneficial relationship with Mr. Bubber, a Jewish businessman in our community who took a liking to me as a young man. I was his son, as he said.

Eventually, we would maintain a great relationship until the day he passed. He was an LSU alumnus with many connections. He made a call and the next thing I knew, I was accepted to Grambling State University on a deal with myself and another student on a football scholarship to be coached and mentored by the late great Eddie Robinson Sr., the winningest coach in college football history. I believe this path was destined for me to cross and was designed perfectly by GOD, no matter how I ended up there.

## *Dear Grambling Ol' Grambling*

Sitting in a room full of extremely talented college athletes puts you under pressure that makes you question your skill sets, abilities, and relevance to the team. Looking around the room and thinking, "Wow, I'm here," is an overwhelming feeling. However, I knew I deserved to be here. I worked hard; blood, sweat, and tears were put on the line to earn this spot. The question was then posed: "Raise your hands if you want to be successful and make it professionally." Out of about 20 guys, all of our hands shot up, including mine. The guys were looking around at each other, trying to determine who wanted it more. I knew in my heart that I did not only want it more; I needed it more. Of course, we all wanted to make it. We all wanted something, but the price we had to pay was not always something we were willing to pay. My position was that there was not anyone in this room who would or could outwork me. The background that I came from, like many of the other athletes in the room, did not allow me the option to give up or not work hard. Not making it was not in my DNA. I needed to prove it to myself and make my family and community proud. It was not an option if I was going to make it or not. I had to make it. The lion in me was ready to devour anyone who stood in my way. This mindset gave me the strength I needed to outwork everyone and excel in all areas of my life. I was always ready to do whatever it took.

I had to take developmental classes at Grambling because my grades were not the best.

This meant I could not play football yet. I could only condition and practice with the team. This meant these developmental classes did not count towards graduation. Which meant I went into college behind the eight ball and had to catch up because of what I did not give precious attention to, my academics in high school.

Coach Robinson started mentoring me. He was a commendable black man of faith and had a way with young men who did not have the example set in front of them. In my case, I had those examples, but there were missing or underdeveloped attributes I needed to attain to be the man I would later transform into. My mother and the rest of my village were assured that he would guide and take care of me. Coach Rob did accomplish what he wanted in me and much more. We had our obstacles, but they were overcome. Like in any healthy mentor relationship, there is a struggle, but it is only because growth is happening.

In 1986, Grambling State University was thriving. Coach Robinson, the football team, the G-Men of Grambling, and the other head coaches in the athletic building made my transition from high school to college smooth. This brotherhood that I was able to establish early on helped my mental space. Coach Robinson and his staff were instrumental in my life. If they knew you had potential, they were always on your back about a particular crippling behavior. One fact that I learned early on about those coaches is that "*I don't know*" was never an acceptable response. We had to be accountable for our actions. They were grooming us for life, not just sports. They wanted to know the thought process behind every action so they could correct it. It was always a correction being made with the team of coaches. The football players had a tight-knit community. We were known as "Rob Boyz," and he took full responsibility for us.

Being a part of a team like this allowed me to thrive. Nonetheless, smooth things often turn rocky.

### *My First Dance Could Have Been My Last Dance*

The first college dance I attended was interesting, to say the least. I was having an amazing time, dancing, vibing to the music, and getting to know a young lady. The entire night, we danced and flirted with each other. My intent was to walk her back to her dorm room. I just knew this was going to be a touchdown. I went to the restroom momentarily, and when I returned, another guy had stepped in. This guy saw me courting her the entire night, but he did not care; he was trying to shoot his shot. The way in which he was conducting himself was inappropriate towards the young lady. He was grinding and gyrating on her on the dance floor. With disdain in my heart, I could not take it anymore, so I said something to him and I slid back in with the young lady for the rest of the night. In fact, I did walk the young lady back to her dorm while we held hands and talked the entire way. I thought the situation at the party was in the rearview mirror. But as soon as I turned around to head to my dorm, the guy was behind me. This brother started threatening me and he had a crew of dudes with him. His ploy, I'm sure, was to kick my ass to make an example of me. I made a split decision to evade these guys. I'm a track star, so I knew they were not going to catch me. When I made it back to the dorm, I told one of the G-Men, and before I knew it, all the football players in the dorm that night teamed up, and we went hunting for those guys. This was Brotherhood. Once we found them, there was little exchange before that first swing, and we started swinging on anybody who we thought was with them. Countless blows were thrown, causing so much damage that a few of those guys had to get dental work and had other major injuries. We sent some of them to the hospital. This was not my intention.

In fact, they wanted to press charges against us; this was a potential lawsuit, but Coach Rob stepped in. Everything at Grambling could have been over had Coach Robinson not stepped in. One small mistake could have landed me back in Gonzales, La, on my back. Coach, in fact, reprimanded us. I thank God for saving us that day. It was almost like he helped us get out of our own way. Coach Robinson's intervention came with physical punishment for our bodies. He made us run the stadium until we threw up our guts. Our pain had to at least touch the surface of what those badly injured guys did or the regret we would have felt had we had to leave Grambling for good. This was retribution.

## *Feelin' Myself*

After my first year, once I completed my developmental classes, I started feeling myself. I felt like I was back in the general population of the student body as far as academics go. I felt like I should be playing football too. This was not the case at all. I was still not playing. Coach Rob saw my inexperience and put me on reserve. My body was conditioned to either play football, basketball, or track during my high school years. Sitting out was not an option, and it never has been. I needed a release, so I started playing intramural basketball with a team named Baton Rouge Metro. This team was exciting, and the student body started coming to the games because we were winning. The head basketball coach, Bob Hopkins, heard about our team and came to one of the games. The coach saw me play and said he wanted me to join Grambling's basketball team, so I did. However, he did a backdoor deal and circumvented Coach Robinson; he should have gone to him first. Coach Robinson was not happy about it. He did not see how I was going to play a sport that I was not on a scholarship for, while maintaining my grades. His stance was that he did not allow his football players to play basketball. But he did, in fact, take several basketball players and convert them to football players, like Ernie Ladd, who ended up playing professional football. But the unspoken rule was that you did not take from Coach Rob. He was powerful at Grambling and around the country. I was strong-willed and rebelled against Coach Rob's better judgment, and played basketball, praying that he would never find out. I was not playing football, so why could I not play basketball? I put in some great work on the basketball court. I worked like a mule. My work ethic was impeccable. I was able to run, jump, and dunk. We had away games often, so I was always traveling around the country with the basketball team, gaining major respect in the basketball world. Coach Rob and I had not had any more conversations; he made himself clear that I was not to play basketball. One rare day, we had a home game. We were shooting around before the game, and guess who was in the stands? Coach Rob, I could have passed out. I did not know if he was going to tell me I could not play or embarrass me in front of the entire gym. I could have frozen like an ice cube. He was just that powerful, and you did not go against the wishes of Coach Eddie Robinson.

After the game, Coach Rob summoned me to his office, and I was certain he was going to make me quit the team. But to my surprise, he started breaking down my game and giving me advice on how to become a better basketball player. He did remind me that I was on a full-ride football scholarship. He then stated that he expected me to keep up with the demands of football and that my grades had to remain above average, if not basketball was over. At the time, there were no student-athletes playing multiple sports at Grambling. This was unheard of. I was so focused on making this work that I studied so hard that I was on the honor roll. I had to prove him wrong and prove to myself that I was capable.

Coach Rob prepared me for life in the NFL more than I can begin to comprehend. The men in my hometown of Gonzales, La, like Mr. Bubber and my Godfather, gave me the foundation I needed to survive in college. Effective community is essential to developing youth at every stage or walk of life.

> *"Glover serves as a role model because he plays three sports and although he sometimes stretches himself thin, he always accomplishes what he sets out to achieve. He is the type of person who will do something and succeed at it, especially when told that he can't do it."*
>
> ~**Aaron James** - *Former NBA player (New Orleans Jazz) and former Head Basketball Coach at Grambling State University*

# CHAPTER 4

# The Man for All Seasons
# (3 Sports Superstar)

### *1988 was pivotal.*

This was the year that helped build my confidence as an athlete. Finally, I understood that both needed to be in alignment to be successful. All those lessons from my Godfather, Mr. Bubber, and Coach Robinson did not fall on deaf ears, as they sometimes may have thought.

The Bible says, "When you find a woman, you find a good thing." In September of 1988, my good thing was located. This sometimes cliché statement is regarded as just that, but it was more than that to me. My now-wife of over 30 years came into my life at a pivotal time. Being a busy athlete who played two sports while trying to juggle a social life stacked up to be a bit much for me. Serial dating at Grambling was easy in 1988. There were about 13 females for every one male. The pickings were plenty, but I had to make the command decision that adding females to the mix would have taken me down a path of distraction. Dating was not going to be beneficial to me. But that day in November of 1988 changed my perspective on that. When I met my future wife, our conversations were just what I needed. She brought structure and stability to my chaotic life. Immediately, I knew she was a woman of value. Before her, I was running back and forth, handling so many different things. She showed me how to be laser-focused. She showed me how to structure my time in a way that allowed me to handle what was important. Even though I told myself I was not going to date anyone exclusively, I made an exception for her. I did not want to lose her. This was not just any old girl at college. This was a quality woman who came from a quality family in Texas. She was going to help me navigate the peaks and valleys of my life at Grambling and beyond. This was a woman I was going to benefit from. Honestly, she took a chance on me because I did not have much to offer her at the time. I was broke, my wardrobe was busted, I was not getting a lot of playing time on the football field and my grades were average. I was not the least qualified or deserving of her. I dated up, and she dated down, essentially. My motive was to get her to understand me while learning about my character, the type of man I was, and the type of man I wanted to become. She was able to see the hardworking and motivated Poncho. She was one of the people who helped push, motivate, and instill confidence to keep me moving forward.

Being with my future wife bred a new Poncho—a more mature, confident Poncho. 1989 was a phenomenal year for me. Talk about a 360-degree turnaround. I was on fire.

Grambling football was exciting then. The stands were going wild. Each time I was called on to deliver, I did. Being a multi-sport athlete had its advantages on the football field; playing basketball allowed me to run very fast and use my height to extend to the line to make a touchdown. The defensive backs were usually shorter than me and did not weigh as much as I did. Our team was very talented, and we had a squad that could play with any of the best teams in the nation. Primarily, my role was to block when called on and score the football when given the chance. Scoring touchdowns on every other ball I caught was what I was known for in college and would also become a big part of my professional career.

One of the biggest football games of the year was the Bayou Classic, a nationally televised game. This event easily drew nearly 75,000 fans to the Superdome in New Orleans. The game had been scheduled a week prior so Grambling could participate in the playoffs. We were victorious over our interstate rival, Southern University, in front of a packed Superdome. This game was one of the most critical of the season, as we earned the right to play in the playoffs. The coaching staff and, of course, the players were elated about what we accomplished, and we planned on taking full advantage of it. Practices and training were all strategically planned and executed. Coach Robinson was one of the best coaches in the country, and we wanted to make certain that our team was represented and respected as well. We had winning on our minds. Everyone on that team gave 110%.

On November 25, 1989, Grambling would face Stephen F. Austin in the playoff game at their home stadium in Nacogdoches, Texas. The 2 1/2-hour drive was thrilling; everyone wanted to win. Testosterone levels were up during the ride there. Upon arriving at the stadium, we could feel the electricity radiating from it. The entire team and coaching staff were hyped and ready to begin our pregame preparation. This game was highly anticipated. The fans, coaching staff, and most importantly, the players knew this game was going to be one for the ages. Grambling was prepared to give the fans a great show, and we did. As a matter of fact, both teams did. That game was certainly a dogfight till the end. We fought back and forth, with both teams taking and losing the lead. This was a nail-biting game. You were sitting on the edge of your seat. If I were a betting man, I would have been stressed watching this game. Both teams played top-tier offense that day. A total of 115 points were scored combined, and the NCAA single-game record yardage was eclipsed on this day. Although I was not a starter in this game, I waited patiently for my opportunity to prove to myself and everyone else that I belonged. Once coach Rob called me in, I took on a new form and displayed a superior performance. This game was a career high for me. My stats were 6 catches, 211 yards, and 3 touchdowns. This game produced my best statistics as a collegiate player. However, it was not good enough to win the game; we lost 59–56. Although the game was lost, I took solace in the fact that the entire team played tooth and nail until the end. The team was disappointed with the loss, but we were still champions in my eyes.

The loss was fuel for my next endeavor. 1989 was going to be my year. I was on the journey to being the best athlete in the country. In just a few days, I was on the basketball court as the starting center. This is how my mind and body were wired. Conquering one thing and then on to the next. Playing football and then transitioning to basketball requires the use of another set of muscles, which was challenging, but I pushed through the pain. It was necessary if I was to succeed in all that I was trying to accomplish. An article was published during that same week in which I received recognition for my contributions on the football field and my seemingly effortless transition to the basketball court. Coach Robinson, being the influential man he was, made some comments about my performance on the football field after that game against Stephen F. Austin, which catapulted me into another stratosphere and garnered attention for me in the professional football arena. At the time, I thought it was honorable of him. Retrospectively, looking back, this was the springboard that I did not know I needed. His words would help get me to the next level. Nonetheless, once all that settled down, I joined the basketball team with aspirations to have the same success on the court as I had on the football field.

## *Committed to Excel*

Just like with anything, there is a process. I had to integrate myself into the team and learn the plays so I could lend my skills to the team. I had little to no tolerance for sitting on the bench, as I had just had enough of that with Coach Robinson and the football team. This meant I had to perform at a high level. Whoever I had to beat to earn playing time was going to get beat; that was my mentality. I was prepared to outwork the best player because I knew I belonged there. The basketball coach had great expectations of me. The coach knew my talent as a basketball player would provide a presence to the team that they did not have at the time. I had the time of my life running, jumping, and dunking the basketball. The basketball highlights and write-ups I'd get were motivation for me to keep outworking my teammates. I had convinced myself that I was not in competition with anyone other than Poncho. I got the opportunity to travel all over the country doing what I loved while sharpening my skill set.

Our team earned great success and was the Southwestern Athletic Conference [SWAC] co-champions with a record of 13-1, tied with our interstate rival Southern University.

In January 1990, Sporting News published an article listing 24 student athletes across the country, including me, who participated in two sports at the collegiate level. I was proud that someone was finally acknowledging the hard work and dedication I was exhibiting in both the classroom and in both sports. These were characteristics my now-girlfriend, Mary, had helped me see in myself prior to this article being published. She believed in me and spoke positively to me. I knew I was talented and proficient enough to achieve this level of athleticism and academia well before it was published in any paper. We were simply waiting for the world to catch up. This was not enough for me since I had mastered these sports. I had an atomic dog mentality. It allowed me to push harder and achieve something no other athlete had at that point achieved: being a successful three-sport athlete and three-sport champion. I can admit that I was a bit ambitious, but that is what it's all about: believing that you can do the impossible and only being in competition with yourself. Besides, it was not like I had not had the blueprint in high school. I was effective at playing three sports at the high school level, so what was preventing me from proving to myself that I could be successful at the collegiate level? Me? With that mindset, I made a decision and joined the track team at Grambling State University.

Cementing my legacy at Grambling State University as one of the most versatile athletes was my goal. After the basketball season was completed, I immediately started training with the guys that ran the quarter mile. I was experienced as a triple jumper, but the sprinter position was on my radar. Again, I had to use another set of muscles. The unbearable amounts of pain my body experienced are unheard of, but it had to be done to attain the amount of triumph I was seeking. Yet the reward is always greater than the sacrifice. I chose to sacrifice.

## *The Trifecta*

The intense training on the track only helped me get faster and stronger as a 6'6 athlete. As time passed, I'd gauge my performance with the world-class sprinters to see where I needed to improve so I could contend at a high level. I was not successful with the sprinters, so I went to the triple jump. At practice, I'd practice jumping with the top triple jump athlete who was on scholarship. He and I worked on our craft, and we soon discovered that I in fact jumped further than he could. Impressed by me, the coach was happy to have me on the team. He was an accomplished coach in track and field, so he knew what skills a track athlete needed to possess. Just like in football and basketball, I earned the opportunity to now travel with the track team to compete across the country. At this point, I had traveled quite a bit across the United States playing sports. During my first track meet at Southern University, I finished in 1st place with a jump of 48 feet, 1 inch, and boy did I feel empowered. This only made me work harder when I returned back to school to prepare for the conference championship. Amid all of this training, my weight was 220 pounds, great for football but not ideal for triple jumping. This meant I was working harder to lift and propel my weight, meaning I put my football and basketball careers at risk of injury. I am a bit hardheaded when it comes to competing, so I pushed harder. The goal was to win a championship in track. If I solidified the triple jump in the conference championship, then I was going to be a three-sport champion, all before graduation. My focus was on the long term. If I had all these accolades on my resume and knew

I wanted to be a professional athlete, it would look more advantageous to the professional teams. Losing was not an option for me. I took this same mentality to the conference championship track meet that was held in Houston, Texas.

Believe it or not, I was not nervous. Adrenaline was flowing through my veins like rushing waterfalls. Invincibility is what I felt. My confidence level was 110%. All I was thinking about was my future and how I needed to perform here today to guarantee myself a bright future as a professional athlete. After the warmups, it was time for the jumps to commence. "Here goes everything, Poncho, do it," is what I thought to myself. After the first attempt, I was in the top three for longest jumps. "Good job, Poncho, do it again; you've got this," is what I told myself. That second jump put me in the lead, and no one could meet or exceed the jump. This 6'6, 220-pound athlete is now a three-sport championship athlete. I was crowned the SWAC Triple Jump Champion that day. My track coach and teammates were both surprised and excited. Can you envision the excitement going on in my brain? I attained a personal goal for myself while being crowned the first three-sport champion athlete at Grambling. With all the hoopla, I decided not to stay and celebrate with my teammates but instead spent time with my girlfriend's family and friends.

1989 was an inconceivable year for my mental, emotional, and physical state. When you tell your mind you can achieve something and you do the work, your body responds, even when it is hard.

Students, teammates, the press, faculty, and coaches alike celebrated my successes all around campus. Articles and chatter around the school calling me a three-sport champion were cool. I became "campus famous" and I was considered a sports superstar.

Playing all those sports for years was starting to catch up to me. I was tired, but my determination to be great and leave satisfied with my accomplishments outweighed those feelings. This last year of basketball was going to shine a light on my basketball skills and strengthen my chances of a professional opportunity. Coach Robinson spoke highly of me again in the papers, which increased my chances of being scouted by the NFL. However, my thought process was to make my portfolio look good on paper, just in case an NFL or NBA recruiter called.

Graduation day at Grambling was emotional and bittersweet. I had traveled a long way from the young man from Gonzales, La, up until now. So much was sacrificed for me to get here. Missing my family, rarely visiting home in the four years, working hard in physical pain to play three different sports, and buckling down on my academics to become a student-athlete were all major sacrifices. Graduation was special, but the work was not over. I still had a year of eligibility to play basketball, so I decided to enroll in graduate school.

*Greater reward, more sacrifice.*

*"Glover's doing a great job for us," Robinson said. "He's a big help to us at the split end position. He's such a solid kid, a big kid who knows his way around a football field as well as a basketball court and a track field. He can catch the ball and go with it, and he presents an inviting target with his size.*

*"Glover's also a good blocker. You have to show a lot of respect for a guy who excels in three sports. To do that, you have to have a tremendous attitude and equally tremendous concentration. He's also an honor student. Man, what more can you ask of an athlete?"*

**~Eddie G Robinson Sr.-** *Former Grambling State University Head Football Coach" winningest coach in college football history", becoming the first coach to record 400 wins. Sent over 200 players to the NFL.*

# CHAPTER 5

# The Godfather's Draft Pick
# [He's Got It]

At Grambling, I had no earthly idea that I was going to play professional football. All I knew to do was play football, basketball, and run track at a high level and be an impact player in all three sports. Rising to the occasion during clutch times. The goal was to be a standout player! I accomplished that title and more.

The day before the NFL draft, April 20th 1991, I was out doing the total opposite of what a potential professional football player should be caught doing. Remember, the NFL was not a guarantee. There was talk that I might get a shot, but I certainly did not rest my hat on it. I was selected to play in an All-Star basketball game, the North vs. South of Louisiana. In hindsight, I was more excited about this game than the draft, and that was simply because it was not 100% that I was going to get that call. There were nearly 20,000 hopeful football players waiting for a call from the

334-pick draft. Getting picked in the draft is like winning the lottery jackpot; it is slim to none. I was going to bet on me. With my mind made up, I opted to play the game. I got the opportunity to start the game; on the tip, the ball was passed to me, and I scored the first shot. This game progressed, and it was by far one of the most competitive basketball games I had played at the collegiate level. The feeling of confidence overcame me because I felt like I belonged among all the all-stars on these teams.

South was playing to the death; this game was intense. It was like they were playing for an opportunity. North maintained at least a five-point lead the entire game. In the last two minutes of the game, South tried to snatch the victory from us, and they were almost successful. A player from the South team knocked down two 3-pointers in the remaining seconds of the game. We were tied with six seconds left in this all-star game. Our coach calls a timeout and draws up a play for our point guard to make the last shot to close out the game with a victory. After we all broke the huddle, we all positioned ourselves and were confident this would play out precisely as it was drawn up for us. The whistle blew. The point guard runs the play to perfection. He goes to the basket, fires off his shot, and misses. I was positioned under the basket and anticipated the miss and I recovered the rebound. With three seconds remaining, I caught the ball coming off the back of the rim and dropped the ball in the basket as time expired. Another impact play, another game-winning bucket. At that moment, I knew I had made my presence felt as one of the best basketball players in Louisiana, and I scored the winning basket. I finished the All-

Star game with 17 points and the winning shot. I wondered if this would lead to a professional career in basketball or if I would get drafted in the NFL in the coming days.

On April 21, 1991, the NFL draft commenced. Two of my high-profile teammates had gotten drafted in the 3rd and 5th rounds. The next day, I was convinced by my girlfriend, Mary, and my mentor to watch the draft on television. I had zero interest in waiting around for a call that might never materialize. I preferred to go fishing, my favorite pastime, to relax. They were both excited that this was even a possibility. My girlfriend, Mary, believed it more than I did. She convinced me not to go fishing.

However, if I was going to make it, I knew it was going to be hard work because nothing was guaranteed. My mentor had been in the trenches with me and had nurtured me into the young man I had become. Again, I did not know my name would be called; I was not even on the top list of players to be called by the NFL. All I was certain of was that I had positioned myself in the best space I knew how as a student and athlete.

The cards were going to fall how they were supposed to. Mary and I waited in anticipation. We sat around talking and having a good time with my mentor and his wife. At this point, a total of four players from Grambling had been drafted. Still no Poncho, still no phone call. The end of the draft was not televised, so I had no idea what round they were on. Now I had to wait for a phone call. The members of my mentor's family had received instructions not to call the house on draft day because we did not want false alarms. When the phone would ring, my heart would race a bit, and the tension in the room would heighten. My mentor would anxiously walk to the phone to answer; once he realized it was a family member trying to see if there was any news, he'd say, "Nothing yet; we must go and keep this line open." My family and hometown were rooting for me, which I was grateful for. That cat-and-mouse game was played a few times with the phone. Through all of this, I was trying to keep my composure and not have too many high hopes. After two days of no calls, I lost a bit of hope. There were 12 rounds and 334 picks. We kept hanging on to pass the time. By the third day, I was in mental anguish. Finally, that phone rang, and it was the secretary of the LA Raiders. My mentor handed me the phone.

"Hi, is this Andrew?"

"Yes," I replied.

"Congratulations, this is the LA Raiders, and you have been drafted."

Everyone in the room yelled with exhilaration! Certainly, she was experienced with families and players screaming with excitement in her ear. Those screams were encased in sacrifices, hard work, hard times, discipline, stress, and much more. After a few seconds, she interjected to say:

"The head coach, Art Shell, wanted to personally congratulate and welcome you to the team."

It was refreshing to speak to him. I learned that he too was an HBCU alum. He expressed how he could not wait to get me to California to get to work. I spoke back to the secretary, and she took all my information and set me up to fly to LA to begin this path that God had created for me. All my hard work, prayers, and support from family members and the community were realized at that moment. What seemed impossible had been made possible by God. It was a surreal moment. I'm a country boy from Louisiana with a one-lane highway who was drafted to the sunny state of California with six lanes going one way. This will be a new world for me. I was the 274th pick in the 10th round of the NFL draft. We celebrated briefly, but I knew the real work would ensue. The call meant I had an opportunity to show the coaches what type of skills I had and why I would be a benefit to their team.

Initially, the thought of going to a big city was overwhelming. But quickly, I realized I had some connections with other football and basketball players that I met and played with in college who lived in California. I was able to lean on those guys to help me get acclimated to the big city and get the lay of the land once I arrived in sunny El Segundo, California. Blue and Red affiliations; I was advised not to go here to minimize my risks. All I wanted to do was play football and focus on making the team. I was still not an official member of the team. This was all conditional. Back then, NFL contracts were not guaranteed. Which translated to: "I did not have time for anything other than making this roster." My focus was laser-sharp, with no room for error.

## *Look Like A Pro*

Once minicamp started, I was informed that my position was being changed from a wide receiver to a tight end and that I was going to have to gain weight. Standing at 220 pounds meant I was too light for that position. They were requiring me to be at least 245 pounds for a tight end position. Immediately, I started on my workouts and diet to get bigger and stronger and learn new techniques as a tight end. Once you sign that contract, you know your time belongs to the team. Your schedule during minicamp and training camp was constricted. Hotels, flights, and all other accommodations were set for you. There is no room for extra, unnecessary activities. Then, if you are picked for the 47-man roster, you are committed from September to January to their set schedule. Those workouts were hell. I had not lifted that much in college, but I was determined to make the team. Each day I lifted and ran. After my workout, I'd purchase a big box of beef, chicken, or shrimp fried rice for like 6 bucks. The shrimp and chicken fried rice were my favorites. I remember pounding down that rice daily. Eat, shower, and sleep, that's what my days consisted of. Then subjected my body to that all over again. I was so locked in to conquering the new challenge that I did not form too many alliances during the camp. I did not consume myself with making too many friends; I kept my mouth shut and watched the veterans. I was determined to make my family, community, wife, and most importantly, myself, proud. Failure was not an option. Nobody was going to outwork me!

The first three days of camp were when all the draft picks came in to see the facilities, learn from the coaches how to line up, where to line up, snap count, playbook, and see how things operated as a LA Raider. Then we were sent home, and the veterans came in for about three days to practice. Finally, when training camp began, we were all meshed together to see how we played as a unit. The veterans knew what they were doing. I had to catch up with my new position and being newly drafted. Thankfully, everyone gave me grace as I transitioned into this new position. They may have given me grace, but I worked arduously. There are 90 men all together, and there is only a 47-man roster to fill. This meant you had to work like a dog, be in sync with your teammates, and learn the playbook. Keep in mind that all these players are the best of the best. We're all jockeying for a spot; no one wants to go home, but some people have to.

Every day we were subjected to stress tests, mentally, physically, and emotionally. Information overload, plays, and performing while you're tired. That was a way to eliminate the ones that were not going to fit with the team dynamic. Errors had to be minimized during this time. You cannot be a distraction of any kind. You had to carry out plays perfectly and keep up with the physical demands. At one point, they put me up against a veteran linebacker who was 240 pounds, while I was 220 pounds. They were trying to discover if I could hold my own and if I could swiftly transition into the player they needed me to be. The pressure was put on me, but if you wanted it, you persevered. If you could win these battles, there was a high probability that you would make the team.

## *Certified Playmaker*

I believed I was going to make it, so I worked hard to make sure it was a reality. After a few weeks into training camp, we packed our bags to head to our first preseason game in Tokyo, Japan, against the Miami Dolphins. Excited was not even the right word to describe how I felt. This young man from Louisiana traveling to Tokyo as a LA Raider was a dream come true. Being an impact player was what I was good at; it was on my mind. I had to make that final roster. Guys were getting cut, and each day you were there, still on the practice field, gave you another chance to prove yourself. Special teams is where I would shine, and I needed to excel in these positions in order to solidify my position on the final team. Things were getting thick. On game day in the Tokyo Dome, I was suited and ready to perform. During the pre-game warmups, all I could think about was what I would do if they gave me a chance. I'm going to prove why I'm here. Patiently, I waited as the first half of the game passed me by. I rooted for my team, but deep down inside, I wanted to be in the game. I knew how to be a team player, even if I was not in the game. This was something I did as a child. I always played the position that needed to be played. Then the third quarter came, and I was given the opportunity to play. All of the veterans had played in the first half of the game and were now sitting on the sidelines. I was waiting on my chance. The offensive coordinator called the play, and it was a play that I recognized. We had practiced this in camp several times. So, my confidence level was high. We all got on the line, and the snap count was called. The line blocked and the quarterback threw a smooth pass, and I got away from the defender to catch the ball. I scored a touchdown in Japan. My first touchdown as a professional NFL player, as a LA Raider, was mesmerizing. It took me back to the feeling I would get catching the multicolored nerf ball on the sandlot in 7th grade. I had aspired to hear my name called by the announcer, and here I was, experiencing this for the first time as a professional. The announcer said "Tatchidaun, Andrew Glover" in Japanese! Wow! God is great, and life is good. I'm grateful for being in the position I was blessed to be in.

Once we arrived in LA, I knew I had to continue to work hard to make the team. Back to my routine of lifting, practicing, and eating fried rice to pack on the muscle to make the weight. I was determined not to allow anyone to outshine me on that football field. I owed myself this. All my hard work in high school and college was not for nothing. It all had a purpose, and it would soon be time to collect. The pressure of waiting to see if your name was going to be called to leave was rough. Can you imagine playing at your best and fighting for your future with other top players with the same mentality? These guys were hopefuls from all around the country, with different backgrounds and personalities. Everybody was a dog, everybody wanted to eat, everybody had a story, and everyone there had dreamed of being a professional football player in the NFL. The dream was realized, but you had to work extra hard. There were only 47 spots, and maybe 40 of them were being filled by the guys who had secured their spots the year before. I had a one-track mind about making the team. Some of those guys were there because they wanted to make it in the NFL; I had to make it in the NFL. I had no other place to go. Traveling back home to Louisiana was not an option for me. It would have been embarrassing for me to go back home empty-handed after sacrificing the last eight years for sports. Simply put, it is not enough to want it; you must possess the mindset that nothing is going to prevent you from getting it. Do what it takes until it is done. These are the things that are going to make your dream a reality.

That number was steadily getting lower. Guys were getting dismissed left and right. I held my own. There were film crews present daily for each walk-through and practice. Everything was under scrutiny, and you were being evaluated at every point by the owners, general managers, and coaches. The eye in the sky doesn't lie. Tardy, dropped. Did not remember plays, dropped. Slacking in workouts, dropped. Not operating well under pressure, dropped. Distractions, dropped. All they needed was a reason to cut you. It was a brutal, dog-eat-dog world. Thank God for a strong support system; my wife was my rock at this time. She saw me at my lowest. She knew I struggled with the insecurity of my abilities. Had it not been for her being there mentally and emotionally, I do not think I would have been able to get through this psychological beat down they took us through. She was the reason I had accomplished what I had thought was humanly impossible in 1989.

This spot had to be secured for Mary, my family, my community, and all my friends rooting for me to win. Based on my draft position, number 274, it was assumed that I would not make the official roster and would remain on the practice teams for the veterans to play against to sharpen their skills. That would not be my story because I believed. I was offered a spot as a LA Raider tight end and signed a $90,000 contract. Boy, I thought I was rich. Coming from nothing to having $90,000 as a salary was a major deal for me. I worked for that money. I played my butt off when I was given the opportunity.

Finally, I was able to move my wife out to LA, and we got an apartment a mile from the practice facilities in El Segundo. I did not want to be too far, and we had a Jeep that we shared. My wife even got a job as a bank teller down the street from our home. I was proud to be able to take care of her to the best of my abilities. She was the woman I had shared $2 nachos with at the student Union at Grambling; we only had $2 between us. I knew I was going to be able to provide the good life that I had promised, and it was only going to get better.

Being in the NFL or any kind of entertainment industry, especially in Los Angeles, brings out the best-looking people. There was a lot of temptation and trouble to get into, but I kept my head down, worked hard, and did not bring any negative attention to the team because I did not want the opportunity to slip through my fingers. I saw too many guys make unsavory decisions and end up losing their money and their families. Lots of times, the women that those guys ended up with were there because of the money. When the money left, the woman left. My agenda was to play football and continue to grow as a player to earn more. I unselfishly contributed to my team for six years as a Raider. Everything that I did I always considered my team. I was asked to play in basketball charities; I played basketball in a gang league to call a truce; I went to hospitals; I volunteered for the Special Olympics; I attended high-profile mixers; and I did many other community-related events with no problem. So much so that in 1994, I was nominated Man of the Year, now called Walter Payton Man of the Year because of my work in the community. When all the players went home in the offseason, I stayed to continue to practice and participate in anything the organization asked of me. Team was my middle name. I wanted to be a Raider. I felt I was doing the right thing by being a team player for the organization, and I believe that is why I was allowed to stay around for six years.

Once you realize your worth, be an advocate for yourself. But be prepared for all that may come with the heat you are about to turn up.

*In ALL ways, advocate for you.*

*"Panchos really started coming on in the last few weeks. He's evolved into a very good blocker and he's catching the ball."*

**~Art Shell-** *NFL Hall of Famer and former football player and coach for the Oakland Raiders. Considered the first African American head coach in modern NFL history.*

# CHAPTER 6

# A Lesson In Loyalty
# and Humility

Many can relate to landing that dream job and being proud of your salary, especially coming from nothing. At last, all my hard work had paid off. With my first salary, I even bought my mother a mobile home at her request. She was owed this and more for her selfless sacrifices. My wife was on hold to get her ring, so we could make that purchase. I financed the mobile home and sacrificed the first two years to pay for this purchase. Coming from where we came from, that meant the world to me and her. She was proud to say her son, Poncho, bought this for me; he was an NFL player.

The phrase "*he plays in the NFL*" meant dollar signs in most people's eyes automatically. My reality was that I only made $90,000 at the time. Family members bombarded me with all sorts of glum stories when I did make it back to Louisiana over the years. These stories always ended with them needing capital from me. You name it, I've heard it. Initially, I felt awkward because my family members were not as fortunate as me financially, so I'd entertain some of those wild stories and give money. Soon after, I then realized I could not take on all the financial burdens of everyone, especially those able-bodied family members who I knew were not going to do the right thing with the funds. It would leave me feeling destitute. However, I had one aunt who I had a special relationship with. Anything she needed, I provided. She looked after me as a boy and sacrificed so much. I owed it to her. Each time I'd visit her, I'd secretly slip a $100 bill in her hand without anyone knowing; this continued until the day she died. Other times, when I felt led to, I'd throw and fund parties to fellowship with my family but leave soon after, leaving all the sad money-motivated stories behind. If I had intentions of maintaining this lifestyle, I had to continue to put in major work and get back to practice. Professional football is a "prove it" sport, so I predominantly stayed in LA to practice my craft, even during the offseason.

One day, I was speaking with one of my teammates, and he showed me his paycheck. Let me tell you, I was flabbergasted, to say the least. Here I was performing at an extremely high level each game, and I was making $90,000 a year. Each Monday, my checks were $4,800. Before I was exposed to what he was making, I thought I was living the dream. $44,000 was my teammates check for one Sunday's game. That bruised my ego. Not to be disrespectful, but my skill set was closely matched with all those guys who made the big salaries. Then I started investigating and chatting with other players, only to find out that the top player in my position was making $1,000,000. I felt swindled. After that, I never opened my own check again. Each Monday, I'd hand over my check to my wife and tell her to handle the business as we discussed. It made me sick to my stomach to look at my check, conscious of the fact that I was at the bottom of the barrel on the pay scale. Not that I was ungrateful for the $90,000, but I knew I deserved more than that. My thought process was that if I'm taking major risks and am as good as or better than others in my position, I should be making $1,000,000 too. I was determined to make that $1,000,000 a year and be labeled one of the top tight ends in the league. I knew my worth. Each year my salary went up in nominal increments; I went from $90k to $100k to $300k, but nothing like how I was valued. NFL salaries were public information, so I was consistently seeing where they were falling short with my pay. Then I told

myself this could not continue, and I was going to get my million. I was brought in the league for a nominal price, so it was going to be hard to get that million. Do not misunderstand me; I worked hard to improve at the position. I did not want handouts, but I wanted what was due to me. Teammates even talked against each other to make sure they secured a spot with the salary they were supposed to make. It was brutal. Some of those guys did not give a damn about winning; all they wanted was playing time, which led to stats and more money for them. This went on for years; it goes on all across the league. These situations were nothing new under the NFL sun, as I came to understand. The NFL is ridiculously competitive.

After I became a starter, during negotiations, my agent spoke to the organization on my behalf. I was offered the opportunity to lock myself into a contract for $600,000. This did not sit well with me, and I decided I'd take a stab at being a free agent. The other guys that were drafted with me in my class took this deal from the Raiders; I did not. I wanted to test the waters in another organization to have the chance to display my talents and improve my stats. Securing a better contract with more money or even more years on a contract. This was my fifth year of being a Raider and contributing to the team.

Amid this, they brought in another tight end, and paid him more. His performance was subpar, and he could not take the starting position from me. Each Sunday, we'd alternate starting; however, he could not dethrone me. Ultimately, he was let go, and they drafted another tight end in the first round. I worked with this player to help him get better and inevitably take my job. The sports reporter asked me what I thought about this new tight end. I said, "If we work together, I think we can both help make the team better by taking on NFL teams." I'd continue to show him the ropes to help him develop as a player. Again, I was being loyal to the team and never spoke ill of anything that was happening inside the organization.

Another position became available because a player was injured. The question was raised about who could play this position. I raised my hand, working for the team and doing whatever it took. There I was, being an impact player, doing what I did, performing, and pivoting to whatever needed to happen. Here I am, 6'6, the tallest player playing a full-back position, which was unheard of during that time. I became a starter doing this lead blocker job, until the starting fullback was healthy enough to return.

The writing was on the wall when they draft your position in the first round. However, I stayed optimistic and played my role. After the '96 season the organization did not offer me a contract.

My agent started shopping me to other teams. I was a free agent. No other team would call me back or was interested in speaking to me. This was a dubious situation; I was young, impeccable at my game, had no issues off the field, and did community work. It did not make sense. After weeks of silence, no one would talk to us. We could not figure out why we could not get any offers. Was it my talent? Was it a slow year financially? By this time, my insecurities about my talents are starting to creep back in. I felt like the insecure player on my junior high school team who was just trying to fit in.

The time with the Raiders shaped me into the player that I would ultimately become. All the resources and time that were poured into me by the organization were much appreciated. I became the player that Al Davis envisioned when he drafted me from Grambling State University in the 10th round. I'm eternally grateful that they called my name in 1991, knowing that thousands of talented players never received the call. The LA Raiders made my dreams as a skinny kid playing football on the sandlot come to fruition. The NFL is very competitive, and I now better understand the choices that needed to be made from a business standpoint.

Thank God I invested the money I was making wisely, because I was unemployed from February until about mid-July. Adjusting to this was difficult because I replayed everything that transpired and wondered if I could have conducted myself differently in the situation. Quickly, I had to realize what happened was out of my control and that I gave110% of myself and was even stretched in some ways. Soon after, I found myself in my mother-in-law's hayloft in Houston, Texas, spending time with my family and my young son. We owned a five-acre ranch home, farm, and home healthcare business.

Running the healthcare business, Glover House, with my family was rewarding. We housed veterans and people with disabilities onsite 24 hours a day. We created a positive, healthy, and relaxing environment for them. This allowed the patients to enjoy the best time of their lives with the time they had left. Alongside that, I did construction around the home and barn, maintained horses, and handled whatever other odd jobs needed to be handled. Truthfully, I had no idea that I would ever play professional football again. However, I did promise myself that if given the opportunity, I would take full advantage of it. Months have passed, and now that it's summertime, I'm adjusting to my new life in Houston. The work we did was rewarding. It was a change of pace from running, jumping, lifting weights, and performing to my limits. With all the work to be done on the ranch, this allowed me the opportunity to keep my body in shape, just in case a call came in.

By this time of year, training camps are now starting in the NFL, and things are looking glum for me. Teams have been picked, and players pretty much know the squad they are working with; they have practiced the playbook religiously at this point. However, there were some problems brewing in Minnesota during training camp. The coaches were complaining about how the tight ends were performing. This is when you insert, BUT GOD!

## MINNESOTA HERE WE COME

The Minnesota opportunity was truly God-sent. I had a former teammate, from Grambling, who was drafted by the Vikings in the 3rd round as a wide receiver in my class. He mentioned my name in a room where a problem was raised and suggested me as the solution. This is a true brotherhood. Given the position, I would have done the same. My friend from Grambling convinced them to call me and give me a shot. They asked him where I was and what I was doing. Meanwhile, my mother-in-law had come to the hayloft, yelling my name at the top of her lungs. We'd just received 50 bales of hay. So, I'm up in the hayloft bailing hay, throwing it left and right to organize and store. Every muscle in my body was working hard. Sweat was pouring from my body and face like a drippy faucet. Hay was in my face, mouth, and hair. As you can imagine, I was a bit alarmed when she called my name from the front door. That was about 30 yards from where I was, standing in the loft. Frustration engulfed me because I could not fathom what she could have needed, especially since she knew what I was doing. Finally, I got down and called back to her. She informed me that I had an important phone call from one of my teammates. They wanted me to come and try out for the Minnesota Vikings to see how I played with their team. She informed them I was in the barn bailing hay. He chuckled momentarily and said he would call me back. Once I got the call back, they asked if I wanted to try out for the team, and I said yes. The team was headed out the next day for a preseason game in Ohio. I was invited to travel to Ohio but declined. Skip the game; I'm not playing in the game; I want the job. Instead, I asked for a couple of days to situate things in Houston. The team booked my flight to Minneapolis.

God made room for me.

## New Team, New Teammates

As soon as they sent the ticket, I was off to the plains of Minnesota to try and grab a spot on the Vikings. This was my only hope. Upon arrival at the training facility at Mankato University, there was no fanfare or a formal meeting with the team. Hurriedly, I took a physical, and they fitted me for my equipment and whisked me onto the field. Sternly, they told me to show them why I deserved the spot on their squad. If not, I was going to be sent back to the farm in Houston. This woke up something in me. I interpreted it as a challenge. This is when my brain would tell my body that it was impact player time. Show them what Poncho can do.

Naturally, I did not think I would be introduced to the team nonchalantly. All the players were already on the field, stretching and talking amongst themselves. The trainer brought me out to the field and paraded me around like a show horse in front of the guys. The players were staring at me like I did not belong and were perplexed as to why I was even there, because technically, I did not belong. All the guys were thinking the same thing. 'What position does he play? I pray it's not mine.' If someone is coming in, somebody has got to leave. Only my college teammate and three others knew why I was there smack in the middle of training camp. God had other plans. The trainer had me jog in front of the guys and then around the field, and then he instructed me to find a place to stretch with the players. There was not one space on the lines because all the guys were sprawled out around like they did not want to let anyone else in. Eventually, I found a spot when my college teammate asked a player to move over so I could slide in to stretch with the team. After we collectively did our light stretch, we broke off into smaller groups to workout with the position coach. This is when everyone discovered what position the mystery man played. Tight end. All the players on the team knew what to do except me. I was trying to keep up, and I'm sure I looked thirsty to be on the field. I was working hard and moving fast. I had to integrate myself into the team. They said they would give me the league minimum of $300,000 and that I had to prove myself in order to have a chance to renegotiate a new contract in the future.

Think about what it would be like if you had to learn plays on the fly during training camp. This is the time when you're supposed to be impressing the coaches. NFL teams have different plays, playbooks, and terminology, so there was no way for me to know their playbook. I'm standing back and watching the team practice plays. The head coach and my position coach are talking and looking at me. Suddenly, my position coach grabbed me by the pads and told me to get in the huddle. The quarterback was not thrilled with me because, when the huddle broke, I was all in his ear, asking him what my assignment was. Obviously, that was the wrong time to ask something like that, but if I did not have some direction, I would cause problems during a play. Those players gave me hell because of that, but I understood. Their sentiment was that this is not the time to have to babysit you and teach you plays. Walking into a well-oiled machine and trying to learn on the fly was not easy. Basically, I had to get in where I fit in, and it had better be the right spot. Performance is key. When the guys saw my grind, they gave me more grace. You must be a dynamic player for your teammates to stop and show you the ropes. A few weeks into camp, one day the head coach asked to see me during training camp. Trepidation must have been written on my face because he told me to relax and that it was not bad news. I'm all too familiar with the "about to get cut from the team" look. They only wanted to let me know that they had observed me working tremendously hard, and they saw what they needed to see in me. I showed the promise of a tight end that they were looking for in the offense, so after each practice, I was required to stay overtime to catch up with the plays. I did not mind because I knew what I was prepared to do: secure a spot on the team. The tight end starter was granted two games to display his talent and claim his spot before they gave me an opportunity at it. Let's just say that by the third game of the season, **I was the starter for the Minnesota Vikings.**

*"He is a very big, agile, fluid receiver with good hands and good speed."*

**~Dennis Green**-*considered the second African American head coach in modern NFL history. He was the Minnesota Vikings head coach from 1992 to 2001.*

# CHAPTER 7

# Declaring Dominion
# (I'm a Viking)

I'm a Viking!

Tried and true!

Nothing is given to you; you must earn it. Earning it is what I did on the Minnesota Vikings team. All teams in the NFL operate with a class system or a ranking system. With me coming in at the last minute, I was certainly at the back of the line. Who starts at the back of the line and works their way to the front of the line in their position. Starting at a disadvantage added searing flames under me to prove why the organization made the right decision by contacting me on that hot summer day as I baled hay in Houston. I'd pushed past four tight ends to make the starting position at Minnesota. They told me to continue to work hard, and they would grant me a new contract. Resoluteness in not allowing this opportunity to slip by me meant extreme focus. I was beginning to change from the inside. Everything I did here had to be calculated and precise because, at any moment, all this could be a memory, as I was now painfully aware of. That meant not rocking the boat and being thankful and humble for the opportunity to play in the NFL again.

In Minnesota, I decided I wanted to become a better version of the person I was meant to be. It was time for me to reflect on my life, redirect my path, and reinvent the man I was becoming. All this would be successfully achieved by rededicating my life to Christ. Being a follower of Christ has been my foundation since I was a kid growing up in Gonzales, La. Rededicating my life to Christ helped me put things into perspective about my life and what was most important. This meant personally, as a husband, a father, a family man, and a professional football player. Major overhauls were my intentions in all those areas; my life was undergoing a renovation in retrospect. Once a week, some of the families and my teammates would gather and have Bible study. This Bible study allowed me to jump leaps and bounds as a man and as a family man. Pressure was applied for me to perform, and that was uncomfortable for me daily, but most of the pressure was intentional. Fumbling this opportunity was not an option; my family was depending on me. A constant cloud of confusion circled over my head, but my relationship with God showed me I was worthy and belonged there. The Bible's teachings allowed us to create a template for success in ourselves, our families, and our careers. Faith, Family and Football.

Spending a significant amount of time with my wife and son was a priority for me. We'd patronize local restaurants and do different activities when I was not working to build a strong family bond. Staying away from the nightlife of Minnesota allowed me to remain centered and focused. I did not spend a lot of time in the city. On Tuesdays, our off day, I'd volunteer my time to do community service work along with some of my teammates.

We'd adopt a great cause and lend our help. In LA, spending a great deal of time with my wife was not always a priority; most weekends I spent with my homeboys that would come up to party with me in El Segundo. Truthfully, I was trying to show them that I had not changed and to show them the life I was living. These weekend outings usually involved me footing the bill, but I did not mind. These were my partners, whom I wanted to succeed in their own lives. Having a big heart allowed me to show them that this life is attainable with hard work. It may not have been football, but hard work breeds this sort of life, which was my motivation. This time around, things had to be different for me to be a better person and not just a football player.

$300,000 was what I was earning in that first year, but $1,000,000 was the contract I desired. I was dedicated and focused, so I put in the work, even though it was hard. During the off-seasons, I would stay extra to hone my skills.

Transforming into the man I was made to be helped me realize this was not just for me: my family was watching how I conducted myself in adversity. My words needed to align with my actions. Words are powerful, and it is important that you always speak with intentionality because you live what you speak. After that first season, I wrote "three years, three million" on my big desk calendar every day and recited it. This was a mantra in my head. When we speak things aloud, our ears hear them, our hearts receive them and then our feet move in that direction. Often, we are not cognizant because we say many things casually.

Whatever you have been saying manifests in your life over time. ALWAYS SPEAK WITH INTENTIONALITY. "Three years, three million. Three years, three million. Three years three million." I said it until I saw what I was praying and working hard for. Shortly after, I was presented with a three-year contract earning $3,000,000 with the Vikings. Often, I ponder: if I had written down three years, six million or ANY million, would that have been my reality? I believe that would have come true too, but I was so focused on attaining that contract because I had been told I would never get the money. God will allow you to settle for the level of life you decide to live. At the time that did not cross my mind. As I grew older, I witnessed how words matter. Sadly, for me, it was a "prove it" point. I proved that I could make $1,000,000. I got my million. A dream was realized. Ask yourself, "What do you have the courage to speak over your life and believe? "Poncho, the $1,000,000 man!" When I tore open my first check, it illuminated the room; it was about $50,000 per week. The feeling was euphoric. I finally earned the salary I had been seeking for seven years in the league. From $90,000 to $1,000,000 over seven years was unheard of then. In your latter years, you usually earn less. On top of that, the average career span in the NFL is three years, and I was in year eight. I was on a thriving trajectory. This was major validation for me, not only for being one of the best tight ends in the league, also for being paid like one. One day this was bound to happen because I had, one, put the work in, and two, believed that it would come to fruition. Statistically, I accomplished more with the Vikings in three years than I did with the Raiders in six years, and I was the fourth or fifth option coming into the season. On top of this, I was 29 years old. Typically, you are given less money when you are older in the NFL because they feel like you slow down, but for me, it was the total opposite. Eternally grateful was my attitude, and I understood this opportunity was from God.

The Vikings team *played* great football. The synergy we had helped us become a dynamic team that effectively worked together and listened to one another on the field. Our bond was deeper than football, our relationships thrived off the field, and it showed. In 1998, we had one of the best seasons in the history of the NFL. That was huge! This was a team that had gelled well and achieved a record of 15-1. This group of men belonged together. A memorable victory was accomplished on January 10, 1999, in the division game against the Arizona Cardinals, 41-21. That was a blowout. We were excited and looking forward to the game that was coming the following week. This was when the letter came from Al Davis. He saw me as the player with the potential he saw at Grambling. Unquestionably, he saw my picture on the cover of USA Today. The picture was not huge, but I was on the cover, nonetheless. His dream for me was realized, but not as a Raider. I believe this is what prompted the letter from him. All eyes were on us, apparently, including Al Davis's. We were on track to go to the Super Bowl with a record like that, and Al believed it too. The Vikings were the highest-scoring offensive team in the NFL, and we had a black head coach and black starting quarterback. History was in the making.

Unfortunately, on January 17, 1999, we lost the NFC championship game against the Atlanta Falcons, 27-30, in overtime. This was the game that determined if your team achieved the ultimate accomplishment in professional football. This NFC championship game had all the players, coaches, and fans from both sides high-strung. It spilled into overtime, but the overtime was not enough for us to score and take the win. However, I was proud of the accomplishments I achieved on the heels of the letter from Al Davis. Being validated, the transitions to the Vikings, my relationship with God, myself, and family—I felt like I had made significant progress.

After three years of being with the Vikings, I was released as a cap casualty. The organization called me in and asked if I was willing to take a pay cut to stay with the team for next year. This was not an option for me. Their justification was that, based on the statistics from the previous year, 1999, I had not met or exceeded expectations. I was told I needed to do more blocking because one of the players was injured, which meant less production. My rebuttal was that I had not been given the same opportunities to play or show my skill set. Respectfully, I declined and never cared to ask about the offer. To be fair, I was in the middle class of salaries on the team at the time; at least 25 guys were making more and could have been asked to take a pay cut. I declined and ultimately it cost me my job. They knew I would not take the pay cut, but it seems to me that asking me to take a pay cut was simpler than cutting me without cause. The writing was on the wall. This was a nice way of saying, "We do not want you anymore." You must be okay with being asked to leave and know where there is a will God will prepare the way.

***There I was, unemployed again!***

"*He's a very unselfish person, and he's a team player.*"

~ **Dave Atkins-***Minnesota Vikings Tight Ends Coach and NFL Coach for 22+ years*

CHAPTER 8

# Who Dat: (Historical Homecoming)

### *Who Dat?! Saint Poncho!*

Back when I was let go from the Oakland Raiders after six years, I was a free agent. Talk of going back home was something my agent and I spoke about often. We had a brief conversation with the New Orleans Saints about me possibly joining the organization then. However, at the time, the New Orleans Saints assured me that they were solid at the tight end position. Not satisfied with their answers, I tried to convince them that they needed my skill set to come in and make the tight end better, but my argument was not enough for them to offer me a contract. It was not time for me to play for my home team. Everything happens at an appointed time, and it was finally time. As fate would have it, I signed with the Minnesota Vikings after that encounter. Customary NFL practices include teams practicing against one another to gauge where each other were.

While I was a Viking, the Saints came up to Minnesota to practice against us one year for about four days. I beat the brakes off those boys. Every time I had an opportunity to make a big play, I gave them the business and caused them all sorts of stress on their defense. After these practice games, reporters wrote about how I annihilated them. Fast forward to the regular season in 1998, when I displayed a paramount game with nine catches. Each play was a clutch play. They knew my abilities well. That performance lingered in their memory, and it would later be what helped me become part of the Saints organization.

Relationship building was something I did well. While meticulously learning each organization, I ingratiated myself with the culture to show I was a hard worker and team player. My best interest was always the team, and this attitude catapulted me into forming beneficial relationships over the years. I also never burned a bridge, and because of this, when a few of the coaches from the Minnesota Vikings were terminated and hired with the New Orleans Saints, I had a way in. As we see, it is advantageous to have people in positions to attest to your work ethic, character, and integrity. The New Orleans Saints had seen me play some time ago and kept me in their back pocket for a time such as this. The New Orleans Saints had a vacancy for a tight end position after being let go from the Minnesota Vikings in 2000. Andrew "Poncho " Glover was named on the list to offer a contract for the position based on his performance against their team back in 1998.

Year ten, and I'm being offered a tight end contract. I expressed to the coaches that the money had to be right. The Saints flew me down and put me up in a hotel. They were signing everyone and getting their contracts in order, but not me. The Saints were scrambling because their record from the year before was 3-13, and they were desperate to build a new, dynamic team. I'm coming off a 15-1 season,2 years earlier. They thought I could be a superior support for the team, but the caveat was that they were going through contracts based on priority. It was taking longer than normal to get the new quarterback signed, which left me like a sitting duck for three days. Apprehension started to creep up because, as I'm thinking now, I'm not a high priority, and I did not want to be brought here to be disappointed.

Finally, I called my agent and said, "*I am not planning to stay in this hotel one more day; either I'm signed or I'm going home.*" Right after that, they offered me a contract for three years and $3,000,000 with a $750,000 bonus to sign, and I accepted it. Instead of signing and faxing the contract back, I hand delivered it to them. All I had to do was wait for that check. This was more money than I had ever signed for, and it was my 10th season in the NFL.

Proudly being able to finally wear the jersey from my hometown was priceless. This experience is indescribable. Family and friends would get to see me live and in color after traveling across the country to play the sport I loved and was introduced to in Gonzales, Louisiana.

I was finally home after years of hard work and dedication. This was a celebration; I told the staff at the Saints that I wanted a press conference to announce my arrival back home. Normally, the team will advise, when you're a high-profile player, that you have a press conference. Then they will prepare for the points and questions that are coming. Shortly after, they advised me that a few reporters from the press wanted to speak to me. They came in, and immediately I told them I was going to give 110% and we would be a winning team. We would give the community something to be proud of. Those words I said were manifested, and we did just that while I was with the Saints.

I was specifically brought in to help the newly drafted starting tight end become an improved player. This has been my track record throughout my career; pushing people to their limits so they can either get better or fold. The coaches instructed me to push him and make it competitive. Motivated by my ambition to prove myself, I saw this as an opportunity to win the position. This is exactly what I accomplished. It took me back to high school and college days, when I would push my teammates beyond their physical limits and have them vomiting and dog tired after running laps around the football field or flights of stairs. Because of my valor and grit, I was named the starter in training camp.

After training camp had concluded, I took time to go to Houston to do some charity work at a school for children. There were only a few weeks before we had to report back to the team for preseason. I had plans to spend the time with my family, work on the farm, and work out in my home gym before the long haul of traveling, games, gruesome schedules, and practices. Eerily, I received a phone call from my position coach, saying I needed to come back now to spend time at the facility. Respectfully, I told him I was not coming back before the season and that I met all requirements, performed damn near perfect, and did everything I was asked. Plus, I had made a commitment to working with the kids at the school, and I was a man of my word. Refusing to come to New Orleans when I was summoned cost me my starting position. They were giving the newly drafted tight end another chance to beat me for the regular season. At this point, I took it in stride. Should I have been livid? Perhaps. Experience has taught me that hard work will outshine any form of mediocre talent any day; alternatively, I played harder. Being in the league for 10 years taught me how to play the game and what politics looked like. The best response to unfairness is to demonstrate how good you are. Back to the competitive-driven games. I worked those guys so hard that I injured my knee right before our first preseason game. It only ended up being a bone bruise and did not require surgery, but it did mean I had to sit out to allow healing. The coaches were getting nervous about me sitting for so long, but I knew I would be able to bounce back successfully. That first preseason game was eventful. The newly drafted tight end who started blew out his Achilles heel. Returning from that first game was humbling for the coaches because now they had to come to me, the veteran tight end, and say, "We need you to take the starting position as the tight end." God has a way of making opportunities come full circle. What is meant for you is for you. The starting position was taken from me but quickly restored. No disrespect to the injured tight end because he healed, but it is a testament to how what is for you will get to you.

*"He doesn't make any mental errors. He's been blocking well, catching the ball pretty good, he's running pretty good."*

~**Jim Haslett**- *Former New Orleans Head Coach,2000-2005*

## *Making History*

Our regular season started with me at the tight end position, and we undoubtedly turned the narrative around from the losing streak of the Saints. My leadership skills shined through with the players, and they respected me. As a veteran, I was able to get through to the guys, and they would listen. I had more influence on the team than I realized, and I believed the organization did not fancy that. One day, my teammates asked me if I would advocate for the team to not pad up through the week. The logic was that we'd perform better by not being worn down, which would consequently allow us to perform better on Sunday with full gear. Surprisingly, the coaches obliged, and sure enough, we had a four-game winning streak. Suddenly, the coaches changed the game and said we had to pad up through the week. Now all the guys are looking at me like I had prior knowledge of this practice change. Honestly, I think small sabotage started happening slowly when I reflect on it. However, we concluded the year with a 10-6 record. We then won the NFC West and advanced to the playoffs for the first time since 1992. The city went nuts. A newspaper headlined "AINT'S NO MORE" with my picture on the front page. The icing on the cake was when we won the first playoff game in the history of the franchise.

"AINT'S NO MORE!" That newspaper article ruffled a few feathers within the organization.

Part of it was because I was not a high-profile player, and they could not fathom me being on the front page. GOD DID IT! Understandably, I thought it was a great look for the team, me being from Louisiana, and our fans.

The words I spoke at that press conference were manifested in atmosphere. Ironically enough, our glory days were halted with a loss in the next round to the Minnesota Vikings.

## *On The Road Again*

Traditionally, your agent is called to notify you on the day of your release from a team. Since I'm a veteran, I am definitely a target. Being the rebellious person I was, I dressed up in a nice business suit and went down to the headquarters office to see the head coach. He needed to look me in the eyes and give an explanation as to why I was losing my job after this historic season. They owed me that. Unfortunately, the players that were brought in to play tight-end were not given a chance to play because of my professionalism, competitiveness, and hard work for the team. My teammates respected me, and the young guys looked up to me, and I served as a mentor where I could. I was there to help them get better. They wanted the younger guys. With the pace and success, I've had in the position, they would have never had an opportunity to play and possibly would have wanted a trade. It was me or them. They chose them. Then the organization gave me the salary cap story. My position was the exact amount they needed to eliminate to be within budget. During that momentous year we had an excess number of incentives paid out. This year the team did well, so the organization was forced to pay out more than the budget could handle because, again, they did not anticipate meeting or exceeding the incentive levels.

I was the target for rectifying the situation. I was heartbroken. I felt like I had been used to get the template for winning and was now deemed dispensable. Before walking out of that office, I said, "*If I'm ever given the opportunity, I'm going to break the Saints back in that game.*" Coach responded, "We know how to take you down from below."

I left that office hurt but confident in my abilities. Back on the farm. Back to Houston. No job – again! But the conversations stayed open with different teams in the NFL. In hindsight, I think I have always been plagued with B or C class representation. I had a good agent, but I had fired previous agents from early days in my career, which proved to be ineffective.

To paint a picture of agent quality, some may have five clients on a team and some may have multiple clients spread across the NFL. Where my agent may have five clients total, of course the other agent can leverage better deals for his clients. The novice agent will not rock the boat because he wants to be able to do future deals with the team. Basically, he takes what he can get for a client, meaning for cheap, just to declare a deal was made. Nonetheless, my agent tried to get me working again based on my experience and reputation.

In the meantime, I was cultivating Glover House with my mother-in-law and wife. While spending that much-needed time with my family. Of course, I stayed in shape just in case my agent was able to get a deal, but we kept getting turned away. At 33, you're a dinosaur in the NFL, and I had already served 10 years in the league with three different teams. Now the conversation is, "What's wrong with him?"

The Pittsburg Stealers allowed me to work out for them. This opportunity came from one of the relationships I established at the New Orleans Saints. One of the staff transferred to upper management at Pittsburg and put my name on the table. I was able to work out with the quarterback, and I believed it was a great workout, but I was never called back.

*"Once a Raider, Always a Raider"*

**~Al Davis-** *Former Principal owner and general manager of the Raiders for 39 years 1972-2011*

# CHAPTER 9

# The Prodigal Son
# Returns Home

Going back to the place where my career started came full circle. It was like playing for the New Orleans Saints, my hometown. After the upset with the Steelers opportunity, my agent called the now-Oakland Raiders later in the preseason during training camp. The Oakland Raiders agreed to sign me to a league minimum contract. I was invited to Oakland to practice in training camp. This is now my 11th training camp experience in the NFL. Once I arrived, the head coach had not received the memo, and his demeanor was rude. It was obvious that I was not welcome on his team. Certain staff, upper management, and trainers that I had a history with welcomed me with open arms. They embraced me and were pleased to see me because I left a positive impact. Al Davis agreed to let me in, but the head coach was in the dark. Identical to Minnesota's training camp, I flew to Oakland for training camp.

Here I am again, walking into a place with no knowledge of what is happening. The coaches and players are trying to figure out why I'm there and who I am. They had little knowledge of my history as a player or character, and from the look on their faces, they were not interested in learning. The head coach was not willing to get me up to speed on the team. He was constantly infuriated with me. I was doomed from the start. This man did not want me to be a part of his team. With that, the head coach repeatedly found flaws and increased expectations of me to devalue my worth and what I brought to the table, but I held my own. During the camp, I received word that one of my former teammates and friend passed away during practice from a heat stroke. He was trying to make weight; he was over 300 pounds and overexerted himself. I wanted to pay my last respects and support my former team and his family. I felt like I had to show my respect, plus all my former teammates were attending. My thought process was to attend the services and come back. Instead of just going to the service on my own merit, I gave the head coach the common respect and asked if I could go on this day trip. This opportunity to get on this team was important for my family and me; I could not fumble it, so again, I asked. He looked me straight in the eyes and said no. His logic was that it was not a good idea to leave since I was trying to make this team; they needed me here. That shattered me. His humanity was questionable from that day forward. After the head coach denied me the right to attend the funeral services, I turned up my game. I was a beast on the field. I turned on Poncho from back in the day, when no one could outrun, work, or play my position. The coaches did not like what I was doing to the team. Noticeably, I paced ahead of my teammates to prove a point. The coaches, especially the head coach, did not appreciate what I was doing. That denial turned a fiery disdain into me; it was my way of rebelling against the "establishment". These bouts of adversity were not new to me, and I pressed on with my best foot forward. Loud whispers in and around the organization provided 80% confidence that I would make the 53-man roster.

## *DOOMSDAY*

The day I was released, I checked out of my hotel earlier than usual to get my day started. During training camps, players are housed in hotels, and once you make the official team, you move into your permanent residence for the season. I'm at the training facility, sitting in the hot tub, getting ready for practice, when I'm notified that it's doomsday for me. Do not pass go. My time was up. I was completely blindsided by this decision and disappointed. In the eleventh hour, it was too late to try and workout for any other teams since there was a cutoff in the NFL, and all teams are now locked in. Other than an injury or extenuating circumstances, nothing else would warrant a late pick-up. Those times are rare. The season starts in 2 weeks, and the 53-man roster is set across the NFL. In hindsight, my only regret was not attending my former teammates' funeral services; I believe the coach was going to cut me from the beginning.

I was released before the regular season started on September 4, 2001. I returned to Houston one week before the regular season began, to be with my family.

On September 11th, 2001, I was with my wife and newborn daughter having breakfast at Denny's. My two older sons were in school. Suddenly, the Twin Towers in New York City had been attacked. Two aircraft were intentionally flown through the buildings. Disbelief was plastered on the faces of everyone in the restaurant. The silence hung over the restaurant like a blanket. At that moment, my world stood motionless. Ten minutes ago, we were just talking about my precious family boarding a plane that day to come and join me. That would have been our reality if I had made the Raiders final roster. Nothing mattered in that moment but the safety and well-being of my family. My wife had secured tickets to fly to Oakland on September 11, 2001. We saw this as a divine intervention from God.

Was football coming to an unexpected halt for me? Exclusively, the NFL traveled by plane. I was not interested in being a part of any copycat situations. The risk was too great for me. My motivation to play football went from 100% to 30%, and based on what we all just witnessed, no one can be sure about anything. What does this mean for my career? What does this mean for my family? What does this mean for the entire country? Everyone in the restaurant is now scrambling and panicking. I hear you, Lord.

Football was still on my radar. Houston had just started a new franchise in 2002. This was my final opportunity. This team was going to need everything since they were brand spanking new. Two things they specifically needed were experience and leadership. I had them both and could help build a thriving organization if given the opportunity. I advised my agent to call the team and sell them on these points, and I was available to play. The team had no interest in signing me because I was 33 years old, and washed up as far as they were concerned. The Texans got beat mercilessly for the first couple of years, because of lack of veteran leadership and lack of experience. What if?

I was done playing in the NFL.

This space is now my dwelling. It was my present truth. I was living, breathing, feeling, and cognizant of the fact that my career as a professional football player was over. By this time of the year, I'm on a team suited and booted. My body kept ordering me to get up. An internal struggle was revving up inside. My body knew I was supposed to be working out for the season, but my mind and heart knew it was over.

For about two weeks, I slept constantly. My mind and body continuously struggled, and it was exhausting. This is nothing I had ever experienced; I slept to no end. I had to rest my body from all those years of constantly pushing its limits and doing it all over again year after year.

Several months later, Al Davis contacted me to see if I had any interest in being an NFL scout and continuing to be a part of the organization. This was not attractive to me because the pay was only $50,000 at best, and this was surely not enough to sustain the lifestyle I had been able to provide for my family. The demanding schedule was not appealing at this point since I had a family. One million to fifty thousand dollars is a drastic change. Respectfully, I declined the offer.

Al Davis allowed me to retire as an Oakland Raider. All my hard work over the years allowed me to have a full-circle moment. Rarely does a player get to retire from the team they started with in the NFL. He had that respect for me to grant this, and I was honored and appreciative.

The line in that letter that read, "Our paths will cross again", makes sense now, years later. **This was the last time I spoke with Al Davis.**

*"Be better today than you were yesterday. Be the one that is going to make a change for the better."*

**Andrew "Poncho" Glover** ~ *Author of G-Man of All Seasons and 10-year NFL Veteran.*

# CHAPTER 10

# The Ambassador (Mentoring the Next Generation)

Football was done. No more painstaking waiting for calls to see if I'm picked up. No more practice. Intense drills. Bright lights. Hits. Catches. Blocks. Throws. Poncho was officially a retired Oakland Raider. Back on the farm in Texas. I was at peace with all that I had accomplished as a professional football player. Money management and planning for the future were things my wife and I took seriously. In my latter years of football, I really honed in on creating a bridge from football to a new life.

One day, my wife and I went to Grambling to visit Coach Robinson. We had not seen each other in years. The first thing he said to me was, "*How are you doing, son? Hell, what are you doing with all that money?*" We were mindful of the fact that the money from the NFL was not going to sustain us forever, but we had a plan that would.

Coach Robinson wanted to ensure that I was prepared for the imminent life waiting around the corner after the big game checks ceased. In true Robinson fashion, he was mentoring me in that brief encounter we had on stewarding the money well. Coach Robinson was correct; we put our heads to the lesson and devised a tight plan. We had grown accustomed to the lifestyle, the big home we built, and all the other perks from the NFL salary, and we had to develop a way to maintain it.

Playing professional football was my only job, so that means no job experience. Nevertheless, my skills attained from childhood on the farm in Gonzales and the farm in Houston, and of course, being a player, gave me some transferable skills to build on.

After officially retiring, we opened three successful Sonic Drive-In restaurants in Houston. Solely operating and owning three locations with over 100 employees was a big piece to bite off, but we did it with confidence—the same confidence I brought to each practice of each sport for each game. The restaurant business is totally different from the NFL, but there are some similarities: Grit, confidence, fortitude, hard work, long hours, being able to pivot quickly, and always operating with excellence with a variety of moving parts. Those moving parts involved myself and my wife literally doing five jobs each to run the business. Countless days passed as I visited all three locations to do maintenance, management, supervision, training, human resources, and everything in between. The payout was rewarding, but the work was tedious and arduous. Those transferable skills of working until I was physically beat but well prepared for a game came in handy many days at these restaurants. Because of my willingness to go hard, we had million-dollar-grossing businesses on the ground in two years following my retirement from professional football.

This next stage of life outside of the home healthcare business and farm had so many possibilities. At this stage of life, I wanted to show my friends and family a different life so they could build wealth for themselves. Giving money to family was something I stopped doing early in my career. My wife had to reel me back in to remind me that I could give it all away. My huge heart was conflicted, but I understood long-term what that would look like for our growing family. Circling back to this idea of helping some family and friends build wealth, my wife and I agreed that we would invite five family members to the ranch to show them hard work, dedication, and what building a business looked like. Meticulously, I handpicked five family members from Louisiana that I thought would benefit from what we were doing to show them a different lifestyle and create a blueprint to build something meaningful and lucrative in their own lives.

One of my cousins, from the five members, went wayward, and I wanted to help him specifically, so I told him he could come down to Houston to work on the farm, help with Glover House, the healthcare business, and live there until I got the Sonic restaurants completely operational. One of my college teammates came out to learn too. He stayed at one of our rental houses next door to my mother-in-law's home, he did odd jobs for the business, and took my mother-in-law to run errands as needed. Once the restaurants were ready, I'd have two of my younger cousins, who lived with me and my family, get up at 4:30 am to drive an hour to go to work with me. I thought if they saw the lifestyle I lived and the work that was put in to attain it, this would benefit them more than just giving them cash in hand. If they could keep up, they would be able to build something on their own, and we'd be able to coexist. If they could not keep up, it was evident they would not be able to help or be of benefit to me in my business. Any thriving business starts with hard work, long days, trial and error, discipline, and consistency. Teaching a man to fish means he will never go hungry, as opposed to giving him a piece of the fish you caught.

Reaching back to my hometown to help family and friends was something I was proud of. This was only possible because I had put myself in a position to have a similar lifestyle as I had in the NFL and understood what the ramifications were if I did not. A couple of these family members and friends I helped went on to be successful. Separation anxiety from everything they knew in Louisiana prevented a couple of them from planting roots in Houston, but I am most proud of the lifestyle others were able to create for themselves after seeing and incorporating the template back home. *You can bring a horse to water, but you cannot make them drink* is a factual cliché because those individuals were not thirsty enough to drink. The people who took the template and applied it were. Those same individuals look up to me now because of the opportunity I gave them.

To be honest, when people reach a certain level of success in life, reaching back to friends and family members is not a common occurrence. There is always the risk of jeopardizing everything you have worked hard to earn. The man I had become allowed me to put those concerns to the side and show my compassion for people. Poncho gave back to his people more than money could ever buy. Being able to accomplish this with the help of my wife and mother-in-law did my heart well.

Mentoring and helping individuals acquire life skills is nothing I'm a stranger to, even before Glover House. While in the NFL, I mentored and gave presentations on life skills and my experiences in colleges, prisons, and hospitals. While playing in Minnesota, I visited New Mexico State, Albany State-New York, and Michigan State, just to name a few to speak to the student athletes about how to get to the NFL and maintain that lifestyle. Currently, I mentor student-athletes, men, women, and children. Everyone has a story to tell. All your unique obstacles and triumphs are to build, motivate, and inspire people on their own journeys. I believe it is my obligation to share my journey to help people avoid or learn from what I have encountered as a man of faith, college athlete,

professional athlete, family man, husband, and successful business owner. When we speak about our journey in a way that grabs the audience's attention, change is bound to happen.

Al Davis's letter was a testament to the evolution of the man I became. During that time, I was not in the same headspace as I am now, but I can appreciate the time and effort to acknowledge the consistent growth. Al Davis realized it before I had an opportunity to fully embrace it. Although he and I never spoke again, I can rest assured that he recognized what he saw early on in that skinny kid from Grambling State University, **The Man For All Seasons!**

# Newspaper Articles & Photo Gallery

## Entitlement Letter from Al Davis

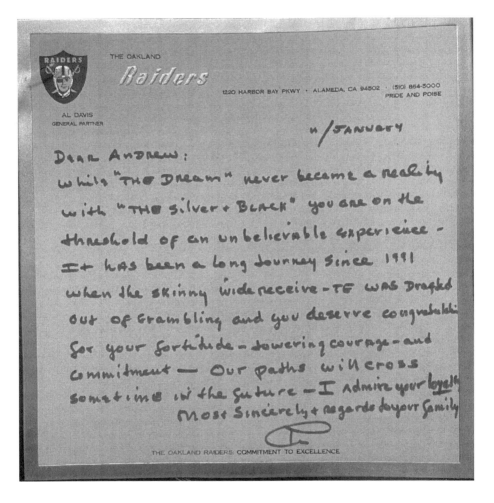

**Tiger Rag • November 16, 1985 • Page 3**

The numerical scale following each player's name indicates where the player ranks at his position and overall among the top 500 players in the country. For example, Top (3-15) means the player is one of three best point guards in the country and one of the 15 best high school seniors in America.

Below is Mike's composite list of the Louisiana players ranked somewhere in the top 500 prospects in the country, followed by top Mississippi players:

1) **Fess Irvin**--5-11, East Ascension High School, Gonzales, PG, Top (3-15).

Heady, multi-talented player, probably purest point guard in class. Size will be only minor college drawback. Despite other reports concerning ACC schools, look for LSU to sign this, their top priority recruit.

2) **Dwayne Bryant**--6-2, De La Salle High School, New Orleans, PG, Top (3-15).

Smart. Great passer who sees court exceptionally well. Committed to Georgetown.

3) **Wayne Sims**--6-6, DeRidder High School, DeRidder, BF, Top (20-100).

Bull inside--can be great scorer when inspired. Moments of domination in state AAU's but disappointed at times at summer national camps. Size may necessitate transition to small forward--cousin of Johnny Jones and, yes, LSU is involved.

4) **Mark Thompson**--6-9, Gueydan High School, Gueydan, BF, Top (50-200).

Great physique; future ahead of him; will be solid power player.

5) **Ben McDonald**--6-6, Denham Springs High. Denham Springs, SF, Top (100-400).

Great all around athlete.

6) **Deron Smith**--6-5, Destrehan High School, Destrehan, SF, Top (100-400).

Another great all-around athlete.

7) **Marvin Lancaster**--6-8, Carrol High School, Monroe, BF, Top (100-500).

Runs floor well, very active inside.

8) **Bryon Taylor**--6-5, John McDonough, New Orleans, SF, Top (100-500).

9) **Juan Hewitt**--6-7, Abramson High School, New Orleans, BF, Top (100-500).

Excelled at AAU and under nationals; on same team with Dwayne Bryant--both all tournament; active for size.

10) **Andrew Glover**--6-6, East Ascension High School, Gonzales, SF, Top (100-500).

Played in Fess Irvin's shadow. Much improved. A real sleeper that should draw attention as year progresses.

11) **Joshua Gilbert**--6-7, New Iberia High School, New Iberia, BF, Top (100-500).

Wiry young man with untapped future potential.

**OTHER DIVISION I PROSPECTS**

12) **Derrick Turner**--6-7, Lake Arthur High School, Lake Arthur, SF.

Physical player, defensive end in football, super sleeper.

13) **Vincent Lee and Victor Lee**--Both 6-6, Minden High School, Minden, SF.

Agile brothers, started on Top 24 team last year.

14) **Eddie Williams**--6-4, Tara High School, Baton Rouge, SF.

Good athlete and swing player.

15) **Brett Guillory**--6-2, LaGrange High School, Lake Charles, PG.

Heady and steady point.

16) **John Simpson**--6-5, St. Thomas Moore High School, Lafayette, 2G.

Good athlete as well as basketball player.

**TOP MISSISSIPPI PROSPECTS**

1) **Andy Kennedy**--6-6, Louisville High School, Louisville, Mississippi, 2G, Top (10-50).

Smooth guard, excellent passer who can also stroke it to 17 feet. Attended LSU summer camp along with Fess Irvin. Priority LSU recruit.

2) **Roger Boyd**--6-9, South Jones High School, Ellisville, C, Top (10-50).

Scores inside with good body position. Intensity is questionable. Committed to Southern Mississippi.

3) **Luther Smith**--6-8, West Tallahatchie High School, Webb, C, Top (100-500).

## Tiger Mile

### State colleges

**MORNING ADVOCATE,**

☐ Tues. Aug. 16, 1988

### Grambling

GRAMBLING — Grambling began two-a-day practices in shorts Monday and Coach Eddie Robinson expressed satisfaction with the physical condition of his squad.

"It appears that the fellows showed up in good shape and that they are enthusiastic and dedicated. It is apparent they have been doing a lot of running on their own," Robinson said.

Early in Monday's drills, it also was apparent Robinson will be stressing timing, execution and fundamentals before the pad work begins Thursday, which is also Media Day.

In the Tiger Mile that kicks off practice, Andrew Glover, a 6-7, 215-pound sophomore split end from Gonzales, had the best time of 5:25.

Others in their order of finish were split end Steven Grant, sophomore from Charles, S.C., 5:30; wingback Fred Jones, senior from Atlanta, Ga., 5:32; wingback Kelsow Williams, sophomore from Cottonport, 5:32, and defensive back Jerome Tullis, junior from Headland, Ala., 5:40.

Tues., Aug. 16, 1988 — **STATE-TIMES**/Baton Rouge, La.

### Grambling

The G-Men began two-a-day practices in shorts Monday.

In the Tiger Mile which kicks off practice, Andrew Glover, a 6-7, 215-pound sophomore split end from East Ascension, placed first at 5:25.

In a 40-yard timing for freshman, redshirts and walk-ons, wingback Jacques Bland has the best time of 4.60.

## Results of Tiger Mile

## Two Sport Recognition Article From Sporting News 1990

THE SPORTING NEWS/JANUARY 22, 1990

**COLLEGE BASKETBALL**

# Two-Sport Athletes Thrive at Virginia

Satisfied with his first-semester grades, Virginia freshman Terry Kirby joined the Cavaliers' basketball team in January. Kirby, the second-leading rusher for the school's football squad, cited a desire to play both sports when he signed a letter of intent with the Cavaliers last winter. Kirby practiced briefly with Virginia's basketball team following the end of the regular season in November, but did not dress for any of the Cavaliers' first nine games.

"That's the way I wanted it," said Kirby, considered the top football player in the country during his senior year in high school. "I didn't want to start basketball until after football season, no matter what. I just wanted to keep my shooting touch. That was all right with (football) Coach (George) Welsh as long as I wasn't playing five-on-five."

Grades had not been posted when Virginia went to Orlando, Fla., for a meeting with Illinois in the Florida Citrus Bowl.

"I talked to (basketball) Coach (Terry) Holland and Coach Welsh, and they know it's academics, football and then basketball," Kirby said. "If my academics are not the way I want them, I'm not going to play. If you have a 1.8 (grade-point average), you're on academic probation, and I don't want to be anywhere near that."

The Cavaliers' basketball coaches think Kirby, a 6-2 guard, could be the kind of player who would play some in every game.

"I hope to play a lot," Kirby said. "It will be demanding. There are so many different defenses and offenses to learn. Hopefully, I can keep my defensive skills up, and that's where I'll get my playing time."

Two of Kirby's teammates "know" football and basketball.

**Terry Kirby**

Quarterback Matt Blundin and tight end Mark Cooke are forwards on the Cavaliers' basketball team.

"Matt was just the heart and soul of our team last year, and we need him," said Holland, in his last season as coach at Virginia before becoming athletic director at Davidson. "But I want him to keep playing football because a lot of people, myself included, think he has a chance to be a pro in that sport."

Popular belief suggests that two-sport athletes at the NCAA Division I level such as the Virginia trio and Middle Tennessee State's Calvin Talford (see story on page 30) are a vanishing breed. But here is an alphabetical listing of other basketball regulars who demonstrate their extraordinary, Bo Jackson can-play-anything-he-wants abilities in intercollegiate or professional sports other than basketball:

■ Maryland's Mike Anderson (football/running back).
■ Washington's Dion Brown (track/long and triple jumper).

■ Connecticut's Scott Burrell (baseball/pitcher).
■ Delaware's Alexander Coles (track/high jumper).
■ Virginia Military's Mark Craft (baseball/pitcher).
■ Grambling State's Andrew Glover (football/split end).
■ Colgate's David Goodwin (football/quarterback).
■ Long Beach State's Rudy Harvey (track/long jumper).
■ Brigham Young's Marty Haws (track/sprinter).
■ Vermont's Rahim Huland El (track/high jumper).
■ Northeast Louisiana's Anthony Jones (track/high jumper).
■ Stanford's Adam Keefe (volleyball).
■ Portland's Josh Lowery (baseball/shortstop in the Philadelphia Phillies' organization).
■ St. Louis' Jeff Luechtefeld (baseball/pitcher and first baseman).
■ Washington's Brent Merritt (track/sprinter).
■ Delaware's Mark Murray (track/sprinter).
■ Missouri's Anthony Peeler (baseball/pitcher, first baseman and outfielder).
■ Northern Iowa's Steve Phyfe (track/high jumper).
■ Cleveland State's Desmond Porter (track/high and triple jumper).
■ Morehead State's Brett Roberts (baseball/pitcher).
■ Manhattan's Peter Runge (baseball/pitcher).
■ Maryland-Baltimore County's Larry Simmons (soccer).
■ East Tennessee State's Calvin Talford (track/high jumper and baseball/outfielder in the Philadelphia Phillies' organization).
■ Nevada-Reno's Matt Williams (track/high jumper).
■ Fairleigh Dickinson's Desi Wilson (baseball/pitcher, first baseman and outfielder).

NOTE: Prize prospects sitting out this season include Brigham Young redshirt Randy Reid (baseball/second baseman), Cleveland State Propo-sition 48 casualty Anthony Reid (track/high jumper) and Cleveland State transfer Mike Wawrzyniak (track/sprinter and high jumper).

## Article From The Times 1990

## Picture Day After Being Crowned 3 Sport Champion

## Presenting Eddie Robinson Sr. With Appreciation Award at My Celebrity Charity Basketball Game at Grambling

## 1990-91 Media Guide

## All-Star Game Article from Advocate 1991

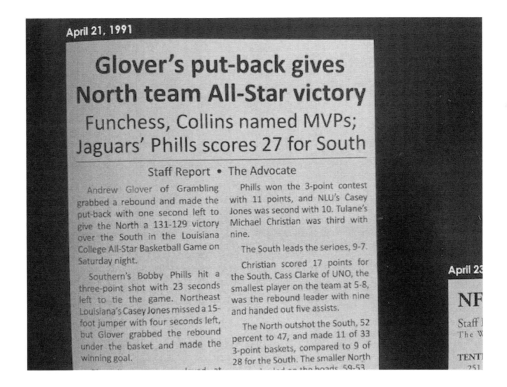

**April 21, 1991**

# Glover's put-back gives North team All-Star victory

## Funchess, Collins named MVPs; Jaguars' Phills scores 27 for South

### Staff Report • The Advocate

Andrew Glover of Grambling grabbed a rebound and made the put-back with one second left to give the North a 131-129 victory over the South in the Louisiana College All-Star Basketball Game on Saturday night.

Southern's Bobby Phills hit a three-point shot with 23 seconds left to tie the game. Northeast Louisiana's Casey Jones missed a 15-foot jumper with four seconds left, but Glover grabbed the rebound under the basket and made the winning goal.

Phills won the 3-point contest with 11 points, and NLU's Casey Jones was second with 10. Tulane's Michael Christian was third with nine.

The South leads the serioes, 9-7.

Christian scored 17 points for the South. Cass Clarke of UNO, the smallest player on the team at 5-8, was the rebound leader with nine and handed out five assists.

The North outshot the South, 52 percent to 47, and made 11 of 33 3-point baskets, compared to 9 of 28 for the South. The smaller North

**April 23**

**NF**

Staff
The W

TENT
251

**Charity Basketball Game with My Raider Teammates**

Basketball Champs@ Santa Clara vs NFL squads.
Raiders Reign! Dey Got Served! #Glover 8782!

## Painting from @ToddMarinovichArt

## First Alley-Oop Slam of College Career

**Graduation Day Dec. 1990 Grambling State University**

## LA Times Article 1994

CARLOS CHAVEZ / Los Angeles Times

Andrew Glover, a 10th-round draft pick in '91, has moved into Raiders' starting lineup at tight end.

'I think that he could be the first two-way player to play professional football and basketball in the same season—he's that good. He would be a legit power forward. He's like Larry Johnson, but he jumps better.'

AUNDRAE RUSSELL
of Southern California Pro League on Andrew Glover

## Man of Year Nomination Article 1995

# "Man Of The Year"
# Raider in the Community

The National Football League's Man of the Year has been a prestigious award given to an active player who excels not only on the field, but in the community as well.

In 1995, this proud program will be even stronger with the support of True-Value as its major sponsor. One of this year's Raider nominees is tight end Andrew Glover.

Andrew Glover's efforts in the community extended nationally. Since his first season with the Raiders he has been working hand in hand with both

Andrew Glover

the Inglewood and Manahattan Beach Police Department D.A.R.E. programs, local Special Olympics and the Watts Summer Games. Andrew was an active member of the "Midnight Madness" basketball league which played a vital roll in the local gang truce by offering friendly competition. Throughout the season Andrew sponsors children in his church, Power of Love Ministry, by offering tickets to games for good graders. 1995 marked the first year an alumni has individually organized a fund raiser for Grambling State University, when

Andrew produced a celebrity basketball game that raised $12,000 for the universities foundation.

Andrew also founded the Glover House in Houston Texas. This project extends a helping hand to the homeless by offering food, clothes and a place to get a new start.

Glover did not miss a start in '94 and he was a valuable weapon on the Raider arsenal. His pure athleticism enables him to hold his own in the trenches while possessing the grace needed to catch a touchdown pass.

## Article from Herald 1996

Friday, November 15, 1996, HERALD

# Raiders' backfield to add new dimension

### 6-7 tight end Glover will also play fullback

**By Bill Soliday**
STAFF WRITER

ALAMEDA — If Derrick Fenner's tender ankle doesn't improve, there's a nasty rumor going around that the Raiders might set some kind of NFL record Sunday night.

Their starting fullback might be 6-foot-7 tight end Andrew Glover. Bingo: the tallest running back to start an NFL game.

Sunday: vs. Minnesota
5 p.m.
TV: none
Radio: 93.3

"That's not a rumor," Glover said. "That's a reality."

The idea of handing the ball up to a running back four inches taller than he is amuses 6-3 quarterback Jeff Hostetler.

"You know, having Poncho back there adds a lot of dimension to us," Hostetler said.

Vertical dimension for sure, only Hostetler was talking about versatility.

"He knows what he is doing," Hostetler said. "He's also a tight end, so he knows about the passing game, routes and protection. I think it's a really good adjustment for us.

"The only thing I worry about is when he sets up to block and is right in front of me. I am definitely not going to see a whole lot."

You may notice no one is saying anything about the 250-pound former starting basketball center at Grambling actually taking a handoff and running into the line.

Glover, who has no carries from scrimmage in his life, isn't campaigning for it.

"A 6-7 fullback?" Glover said,

wincing. "That leaves a lot of room to be hit and I'd rather do the hitting than get hit."

Coach Mike White jokes that 320-pound defensive tackle Jerry Ball, who sometimes plays fullback in goal-line situations, will get the ball before Glover does.

Hostetler isn't so sure.

"You never know," he said with a wicked grin. "Especially in no-huddle you never know who is going to get the ball."

"He just might," White said, adding he hoped Glover would know what direction to go.

Please see Raiders, 9-14

- 123 -

## Hall of Fame Weekend Photo-Pic

## Hall Of Fame Plaque

## Visiting Statue in Eddie Robinson Sr. Museum

Da Legend! Follow me Pro Player Promotions! We here, We there, We everywhere u wanna Be! #Glover8782.

**EHBC Basketball History & Legends HBCU**

Anderson- Gale    Glover – Loder

Lorthridge – Short      Sillmon – Young

**Andrew GLOVER**
Grambling State

## LA Raiders Rookie photo 1991

ANDREW GLOVER    TE    LOS ANGELES RAIDERS

**Spike After Touchdown Against Cleveland Browns LA Coliseum**

Made in the USA
Columbia, SC
16 May 2024

35391560R00072